100

THINGS TO DO IN BOSTON BEFORE YOU DIE

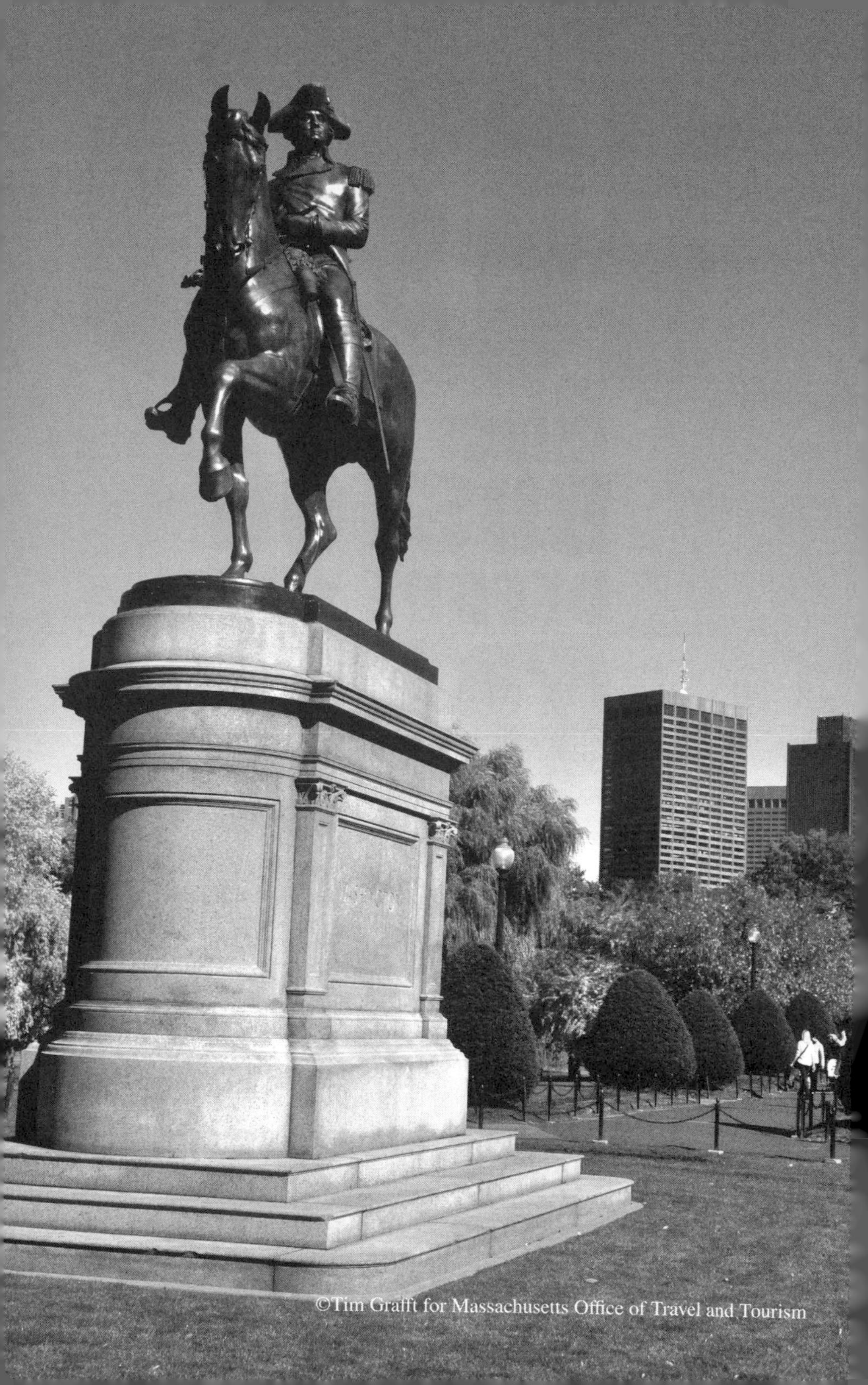

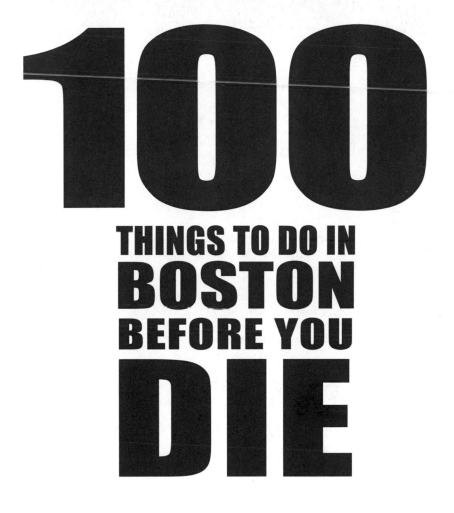

100
THINGS TO DO IN
BOSTON
BEFORE YOU
DIE

LEIGH HARRINGTON

REEDY PRESS

Library of Congress Control Number: 2015942713

ISBN: 9781681060118

Design by Jill Halpin

Cover Image: ©Alexandra Molnar for Massachusetts Office of Travel and Tourism

Printed in the United States of America
15 16 17 18 19   5 4 3 2 1

Please note that websites, phone numbers, addresses, and company names are subject to change or cancellation. We did our best to relay the most accurate information available, but due to circumstances beyond our control, please do not hold us liable for misinformation. When exploring new destinations, please do your homework before you go.

CONTENTS

PREFACE

If you're reading this book, you're either a traveler who's come to experience this amazing city called Boston, or you live here already and are looking to get better acquainted with your hometown.

Either way, you've come to the right place.

You're holding in your hands 100 solid reasons to stop saying, "I should go do that sometime," and actually go do it. This is a bucket list of sorts, a Boston tutorial and a go-to guide for all things fun. Dog-ear the pages, take notes, rough it up in your backpack or purse. Use it, and then use it again, and again, and again.

A few things to note: Boston is a smaller city (considering other major cities like Chicago or LA) chock full of things to do. Items included in this book are situated within an approximate five-mile radius of Boston proper, but might also be in Cambridge, Brookline and Somerville, each its own city that collectively falls under the umbrella of "The Hub."

Upon venturing out to explore Boston, I suggest calling ahead to confirm details. While all information is accurate at this moment, things do change.

• •

Follow me @lahlah_land on Twitter and @lahlah_landpix on Instagram to learn about many more things to do in Boston.

Good luck!

Leigh Harrington
May 2015

ACKNOWLEDGMENTS

I'd still be trying to narrow all the wonderful things about Boston down to just 100 were it not for my friends, family and colleagues who offered voices of reason throughout this process and the lucky ones who got to accompany me on "research" trips. Thanks to Mat for showing me around Chinatown, and to Eric, Dan, Babs and Jon for the insightful editing. Thanks to Amanda for bringing this opportunity to my attention! Most of all, thank you to my darling Violet for keeping me sane, and to John for your tremendous encouragement and support.

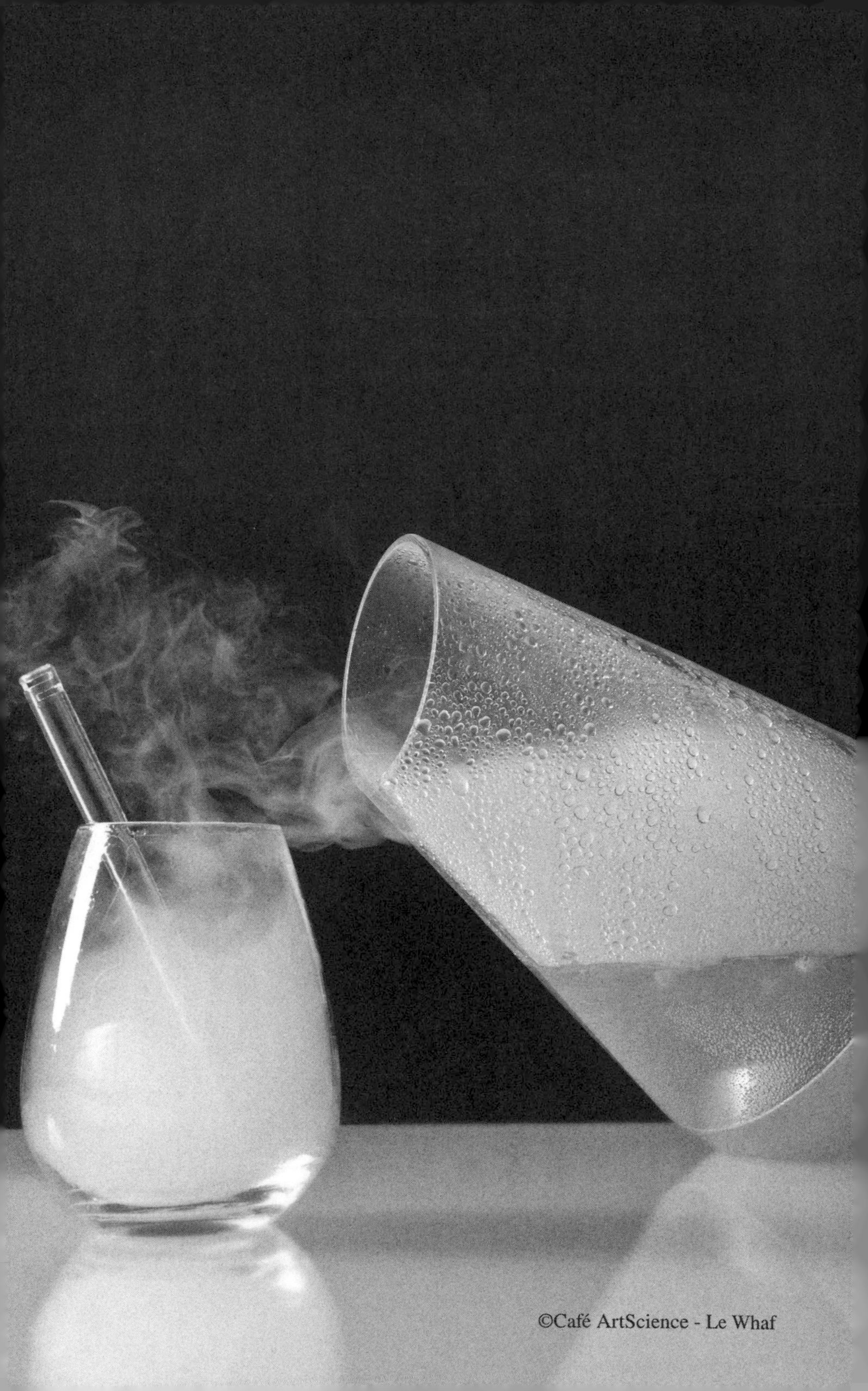

©Café ArtScience - Le Whaf

FOOD AND
DRINK

EAT
INDIAN PUDDING, BAKED BEANS, AND PRIME RIB AT A CENTURIES-OLD RESTAURANT

What's Boston without its Colonial history? Buffs score big in this town because here you can really dine like an early Yankee. Strap on your sneakers for walking on cobblestones and pick up the Freedom Trail near Haymarket, then follow it past the Bell in Hand Tavern, the Union Oyster House, Faneuil Hall, and into Faneuil Hall Marketplace, where Durgin-Park beckons to the left. The place earned its existing name in 1825, but the space has been serving food to market vendors, merchants, and hungry sailors since 1742. In a lively, open dining room, friendly but frank waitresses drop cornbread at wooden market tables draped in red-checkered tablecloths. Customers range from out-of-towners to Financial District regulars—the place may be a tourist trap, but the food is good. Highlights of the menu are tried-and-true regional favorites: roast prime rib, savory pot roast in gravy, baked Boston scrod, and the most molasses-y baked beans you've ever had. Save room for dessert, because you'll probably never see Indian pudding on the menu anywhere else. This mushy, piping hot treat is a hybrid of British culinary tradition and ingredients native to the New World; it's a cornmeal-and-molasses-infused porridge served with a scoop of vanilla ice cream on top.

340 Faneuil Hall, Boston, 617-227-2038
www.arkrestaurants.com/durgin-park

EAT
OYSTERS AND CHOWDER AT ANOTHER CENTURIES-OLD RESTAURANT

A National Historic Landmark, Union Oyster House officially holds the title of the "oldest continually operated restaurant and oyster bar in the United States." So, obviously, you must try the oysters here. The circular downstairs bar is the place to order some freshly shucked, as well as steamers and/or mussels. You can say you ate in the same spot where Daniel Webster was famously known to dine daily. Upstairs, dig into fried oysters, fish chowder, and lobster served no less than six different ways. JFK loved eating here so much that he earned his own dedicated booth today marked with a plaque. But, food's not the only thing to note while visiting Union Oyster House: curiously, it's the first place in the country where toothpicks were used; the site once served as the home of King Louis-Philippe I, the last King of France; and the Revolutionary-era rag the *Massachusetts Spy* was printed here.

41 Union St., Boston, 617-227-2750
www.unionoysterhouse.com

HAVE DINNER
AT JOHN HANCOCK'S PLACE

Built in 1763, the gray-shuttered brick Gardiner Building is Long Wharf's oldest building. It's also the Chart House, a sophisticated seafood restaurant with a number of locations across the country. Yes, you're here to eat (try the lobster-stuffed scrod or the beer steamed mussels), but first we must appreciate this place's history. It was merchant (smuggler) and noted patriot John Hancock's counting house, where he unloaded imported goods from his ships, like the *Liberty*. Today, the building retains many of its original fixtures from the Revolutionary era: its brick walls and wood beam ceiling, its staircase, and Hancock's safe.

60 Long Wharf, Boston, 617-227-1576
www.chart-house.com

GET HOOKED
ON A LOBSTER ROLL

Did you know that in the Colonial era, lobster was so unpopular as a food that it was fed to prisoners and indentured servants and was even used as fish bait? Not so today. In fact, just the opposite: fans of New England's native crustacean pay hefty sums for a turn at cracking a claw and swiping it through melted butter. But I'm talking here about another popular way this region eats lobster meat—in roll form, slathered in mayonnaise and stuffed into a hot dog bun. Variations on mayo-to-meat ratio, celery or no celery, salt, pepper, and other spices range from restaurant to lobster shack, but for a lobster roll that nears perfection, head to James Hook at Atlantic and Northern avenues. You can't miss the family-owned company's brown wooden retail shop, since it stands out among the skyscrapers of the Financial District. There are a few seats inside, but otherwise you're taking this roll to go.

15 Northern Ave., Boston, 617-423-5501
www.jameshooklobster.com

CHEER FOR BEER
AT HARPOON BREWERY

Belly up to the bar at Harpoon Brewery's Beer Hall the next time you have a hankering for an afternoon pint. The local-turned-national brand features many of its signatures fresh on tap, including its UFO line, its Leviathan IPA, and a rotating selection of pilot beers, all served in flavor-enhancing glassware. Equal opportunity drinkers can order a flight. Hungry? The Beer Hall doesn't operate a full-service kitchen, but hot pretzels with sauces like Rye Jack cheese and maple cider icing are available for those who need a little something. If you've got a tot in tow, Harpoon has its own buttery root beer on draft, but note that on Saturdays the Beer Hall is strictly 21+.

306 Northern Ave., Boston, 617-456-2322
www.harpoonbrewery.com

TIP

Because the Beer Hall is located within Harpoon's headquarters, this is a great time to take a brewery tour and learn the nuts and bolts of beer production. The tour costs $5 and includes samples.

BOSTON BREWERY TOURS AND TASTING ROOMS

Aeronaut Brewing Co.
14 Tyler St., Somerville, 617-987-4236

Bantam Cider Company
40 Merriam St., Somerville, 617-299-8600

Harpoon Brewery
306 Northern Ave., Boston, 617-456-2322

Samuel Adams Brewery
30 Germania St., Boston, 617-368-5080

Somerville Brewing Company
15 Ward St., Somerville, 617-764-0578

Trillium Brewing Company
369 Congress St., Boston, 617-453-8745

EAT YOUR WAY
THROUGH CHINATOWN

Boston's Chinatown is a mix of Old World and New World tradition from America and the Far East. If you're a lover of Asian cuisine, plan to bank some time in this neighborhood that has it all, from Korean fried chicken to Japanese hot pot. But before you let your belly go hog-wild, get down to basics on this self-guided gastronomic adventure to my picks for best Chinese joints—it is named Chinatown, after all.

Dumpling Cafe
You'll end up sharing a table at this Taiwanese place that looks like a hole in the wall but is actually one of Chinatown's hottest stops for dumplings. What you'll order here: insanely plump roasted duck buns as well as *xiaolongbao* soup dumplings—they're filled with broth, and your job is to slurp it out, not have it run down your chin.

695 Washington St., Boston, 617-338-8858
www.dumplingcafe.com

Hong Kong Eatery
This Chinese quick-hit is famous for two things: barbecued meats—which dangle in the front window unless they're sold out for the day—and whopping portions of wonton soup: a savory pork broth swimming with scallions, leeks, and dangerously obese shrimp dumplings.

79 Harrison Ave., Boston, 617-423-0838
www.hongkongeatery.com

Peach Farm

Julia Child enjoyed eating at this Cantonese landmark, where diners order fish fresh out of the tank, which means one minute it's swimming and the next, it's steaming. Also order the house fried rice with sweet Chinese sausage and scallops.

4 Tyler St., Boston, 617-482-3332
www.peachfarmboston.com

New Shanghai

Don't be fooled by this misnomer; Szechuan cuisine is what you'll dig into here. Spicy, peanut-loaded kung pao chicken is a classic of the region and a signature of this restaurant. Snack on the cumin lamb, another specialty, and then cool the palate with cucumbers in minced scallion sauce.

21 Hudson St., Boston, 617-338-6688
www.bostonjingchuanjiujia.com

China King

Plan ahead for a meal at China King and then bring your appetite: you must order the Peking Duck one day in advance. If you happen to be walking by, stop in for the scallion pancakes.

60 Beach St., Boston, 617-542-1763

Great Taste Bakery

End your impromptu tour through Chinatown with something sweet. Eggy custard fills the popular Portuguese tart, a Chinese classic so named because of Portugal's influence in Hong Kong and Macau in the 1940s.

61-63 Beach St., Boston, 617-426-8899
www.greattasteboston.com

GO NUTS
FOR THINKING CUP'S HAZELNUT LATTE

When it comes to coffee, Boston doesn't ever claim to be Seattle, Portland, or even New York, despite what its curious nickname—Beantown—seemingly implies. (In actuality, the moniker derives from the regional culinary staple, baked beans.) We don't mean to say that Boston is without a counter culture. Urban hipster hotspot Thinking Cup elevates expectations of what coffee can and should be, transforming roasted Stumptown coffee beans into carefully crafted espresso drinks. Thinking Cup's hazelnut latte is a must for its freshly roasted hazelnut paste that leaves bits of the real thing on the tongue, its bold, sophisticated flavor profile, and its jolt of caffeine to which Dunkin' Donuts regulars definitely aren't accustomed.

85 Newbury St., Boston, 617-247-3333
165 Tremont St., Boston, 617-482-5555
236 Hanover St., Boston, 857-233-5277
www.thinkingcup.com

SPOIL YOURSELF
WITH SMALL PLATES AT COPPA

Beef heart pastrami, duck prosciutto, mortadella: there's a whole section of the menu at COPPA devoted to charcuterie that chef-owner Jamie Bissonnette lovingly seeks out from purveyors right here in Massachusetts. Let your appetite explore these meaty marvels, but don't stop the ordering there. The kitchen sources local sustainable and artisanal ingredients, packing each dish with a punch of flavor despite being diminutively sized. COPPA's menu changes seasonally, so each visit guarantees a fresh experience. Bissonnette has been known to do such things as dress wood-oven charred cauliflower with fresh mint leaves, peppery olive oil, yogurt, and lemon. One hit that never leaves: the wood-fired Salsiccia pizza studded with tomatoes and ricotta, pork sausage, roasted onions, and fennel pollen. It's no wonder this charming corner eatery with its 2014 James Beard Award-winning Best Chef is a go-to for South Enders.

253 Shawmut Ave., Boston, 617-391-0902
www.coppaboston.com

GRAB GARLIC KNOTS
AT AREA FOUR

So you are reading this and saying to yourself, "Seriously? This chick is sending me to Kendall Square for garlic knots?" Well, yes. Yes, I am. The sinful version baked up by Jeff Pond at Michael Leviton's contemporary pizzeria, Area Four, is beyond compare and has been a staple on the menu since shortly after opening in 2011. Pond kneads raw pizza crust—made from a twelve-year-old sourdough starter—into doughy dumplings that get fired in a cast iron pan inside the restaurant's wood-burning oven. If you choose to make your order a "supreme" (do it, I dare you), the buttery, garlicky knots come served swimming in red sauce and smothered in fontina, pecorino, and house-made mozzarella cheese.

500 Technology Square, Cambridge, 617-758-4444

www.areafour.com

TIP

Don't overlook Area Four's chewy hewy pizza—the closest comparison would be Neapolitan-style—it's some of the best in town. Along with the ever-changing menu of toppings, there's the not-on-the-menu "secret" pizza topped with soppressata, pickled banana peppers, basil, and cracked eggs.

BITE
INTO A BARTLEY'S BURGER

There are plenty of places in Harvard Square to get a burger, but the joint where you should get one has been a local landmark since 1960. Mr. Bartley's Gourmet Burgers is known for its mile-long menu of styles gamely named for current trends (the Hashtag, with #boursinandbacon), world leaders (the "attack your taste buds" Putin), and headline-grabbing celebrities (the teriyaki-pineapple-topped Kim Kardashian). Blackened and crispy on the outside, with a juicy pink center, these patties are ground fresh daily and weigh in at seven ounces. Platters are huge, considering the heaping sides of french fries, sweet potato fries (award-winning), or crumbly hand-breaded onion rings (also award-winning). Mr. Bartley's atmosphere is as curious as its menu: decor includes an Elvis bust, an inflatable buck head, and an assortment of tattered concert posters and other delightfully awful wall art. The only potential drawbacks are the sometimes-long-but-fast-moving line to get in, the cash-only policy, and the jam-packed seating; but hey, strike up a conversation with your neighbor. With Harvard University right across the street, you never know who it might be.

1246 Massachusetts Ave., Cambridge, 617-354-6559
www.mrbartley.com

MUNCH ON BRUNCH
AT HENRIETTA'S TABLE

Before you jump to any conclusions about the "hotel buffet brunch" I'm about to recommend, please understand that the Sunday spread put forth by Executive Chef Peter Davis at Henrietta's Table at the Charles Hotel is simply no ordinary hotel buffet brunch. After fifteen years, it tends to fly under the radar of current "Best of" lists, but for those in the know (some of whom are quite notable—think Harvard) it remains a cozy, convivial favorite. There's the cold salad table laden with mushroom salad and ziti with feta and platters of roasted carrots, asparagus, zucchini, or whatever vegetables happen to be in season— Davis makes it his mission to source ingredients from local farmers. There's cheese for every fan, from hearty slabs of Grafton cheddar to artisanal Hannahbells made at Shy Brothers Farm in Westport. There are shrimp cocktail and raw oysters and a half-dozen paté varieties with garnishes. There are hot entrees, like mahimahi, or roasted chicken with three-cheese mashed potatoes. There are made-to-order omelets, waffles, and a rib-eye roast carved on the spot. And then there's dessert: slices of flourless chocolate cake, apple-cranberry cobbler, sturdy Key lime pie, and raspberry cream puffs. Hooked yet? Bring your appetite and fifty bucks—I didn't say it was cheap.

Sundays noon-3 pm

1 Bennett St., Cambridge, 617-661-5005
www.henriettastable.com

GO ALL IN
AT TASTY BURGER

Speaking of burgers, it's not worth watching your waistline during a visit to Tasty Burger in the Fenway, where the grub may be cheap but sure is delicious. Dave Dubois' retro-styled, fast-food fantasyland serves up loaded—and we mean loaded—humanely raised beef in one-third-pound burgers topped with melted blue cheese, or battered and fried and slathered in spicy-sweet relish. Quarter-pound franks, made in-house and called Shafts, get equal treatment, and if you think you can eat three souped-up versions in under an hour, then we'd love to see you take the Tasty Burger Challenge. Our pick for best meal in the house: the Butta Burger drenched in melting butter and caramelized onions, paired with an order of French fries smothered in homemade cheese sauce and creamy sausage gravy.

1301 Boylston St., Boston, 617-425-4444
40 JFK St., Cambridge
69 L St., South Boston (limited menu; take-out only)
www.tastyburger.com

TIP

Any Boston resident holding
a valid student ID can snag the
"Starvin' Student" deal: a hamburger or
cheeseburger, fries, and a beer for the
bargain price of ten bucks.

OVERDOSE ON CHOCOLATE
AT THE LANGHAM ...

For more than a quarter century, this Financial District luxury hotel has been encouraging its guests to mainline chocolate on Saturday afternoons. The famed Chocolate Bar is a sweets addict's dream come true, with 200 pounds of white, milk, and dark turned into decadent, bite-sized desserts. Pastry creations might appear as a caramel chocolate mousse bombe, bacon banana tart, or white chocolate pistachio tart, but the overall theme reflects the season and changes annually. Besides all that, there's a dip-it-yourself chocolate fountain, molten lava cakes to-order, a homemade ice cream and mix-in station, custom chocolate-fruit crepes, cotton candy, and, for the twenty-one-plus crowd, deliciously boozy chocolate cocktails.

September through June

The Langham, Boston, 250 Franklin St., Boston, 617-451-1900
www.langhamhotels.com

TIP

Arrive early for your reservation and bide a few minutes in the Wyeth Room for a peek at two large-scale, original oil murals by N.C. Wyeth (father of Andrew Wyeth and grandfather of Jamie Wyeth, both realist painters themselves). The works were created to fit this precise space, formerly the Federal Reserve Bank of Boston.

...THEN
SEEK OUT CHOCOLATE THERAPY

"Fantastic, That's You" by Benny Carter and His Orchestra trickles lightly through the air at Back Bay's L.A. Burdick chocolate shop, where you're stopping in for a cup of hot chocolate even if you're caught in the middle of the Northeast's sweaty summer months. There's an elegant European patrician vibe, complete with gold, pink, and sage stripes painted on the walls and a swooping brass chandelier hanging from the ceiling. Although it'll be a bit rich, for both the palate and the wallet, I recommend trying all three signature styles, made with tasty gourmet cocoa from South and Central America, and the Caribbean. You're here, so why not? White chocolate is creamy, buttery, and aromatic, with fresh nutmeg shaved on top. Tangy and sweet describes the uber popular milk chocolate, while the dark chocolate boasts a you-love-it-or-you-don't character that's bitter like a jealous ex. Sip inside rather than taking your cup to go—there's something about having it served table-side in a ceramic cup and saucer that completes your quest.

220 Clarendon St., Boston, 617-303-0113
52 Brattle St., Cambridge, 617-491-4340
www.burdickchocolate.com

BE THE YANKEE
AT THE BBQ

Roll up your sleeves, lick your lips, and dig into St. Louis ribs, beef brisket, or buttermilk fried chicken at Tiffani Faison's Texas-style barbecue joint, Sweet Cheeks Q. This Fenway neighborhood hot spot features elevated renditions of down-home cooking, using all-natural meats and house-made everything, including its Memphis-style barbecue sauce. Order by the tray or the sandwich, plated with hot and cold scoops of carrot raisin salad or broccoli cheese casserole served in royal blue enamelware. Don't forget to order a biscuit with honey butter—there's a reason they're three bucks a pop. If you don't have other plans for the evening, I recommend sticking around for a mason jar cocktail or an Evan Williams single barrel bourbon, neat.

1381 Boylston St., 617-266-1300
www.sweetcheeksq.com

DIVE DEEP
INTO BAKED RIGATONI

Bubbling beneath its crunchy crust of broiled Parmesan and served in an ample cast iron Staub cocotte, Eastern Standard's signature dish is one for the ages. Proprietor Garrett Harker and opening chef Jamie Bissonnette (yes, we have talked about him already—he's partner and chef at COPPA, page 11) collaborated on this pasta dish when the place first launched a decade ago. It is meant to be a French-ish modification of a traditionally Italian preparation. Everything is made in-house from scratch, of course, even its individual components: crumbly lamb and pork-butt sausage, ricotta cheese, and its velvety pink sauce, rich with tomatoes and cream. Toss in some peas, basil, and nutmeg, and you've got one seriously decadent, ridiculously delicious concoction that's a challenge to finish in one sitting. Not that anyone's keeping count, but as of the end of 2014, the baked rigatoni had been ordered 57,000 times.

I told you: it's that good.

528 Commonwealth Ave., Boston, 617-532-9100
www.easternstandardboston.com

TIP

If you can manage dessert, order another ES signature: the butterscotch bread pudding. It's been on the menu almost as long as the rigatoni and is nearly as decadent—a warm, buttery brioche topped with praline ice cream and a sticky salted caramel sauce.

STAKE OUT
A CELEBRITY CHEF

Boston might not cultivate as many celebrity-chef-driven restaurants as, say, New York or LA, but where food is concerned you've just got to choose quality over quantity. So the next time you're hankering for an absolutely delicious meal, stake out local kitchens run by Boston-based "Top Chef," "Hell's Kitchen," "Iron Chef," and/or Food Network alums, who follow in the footsteps of the woman who is arguably the country's first chef-lebrity, Julia Child. She launched her legacy right here on WGBH with her show *The French Chef*.

Jody Adams at Rialto
1 Bennett St., Cambridge, 617-661-5050
www.rialto-restaurant.com

Tiffani Faison at Sweet Cheeks Q
1381 Boylston St., Boston, 617-266-1300
www.sweetcheeksq.com

Barbara Lynch at No. 9 Park
9 Park St., Boston, 617-742-9991
www.no9park.com

Ken Oringer at Clio
370A Commonwealth Ave., 617-536-7200
www.cliorestaurant.com

Jason Santos at Abby Lane
255 Tremont St., Boston, 617-451-2229
www.abbylaneboston.com

Michael Schlow at Tico
222 Berkeley St., 617-351-0400
www.ticoboston.com

Ming Tsai at Blue Dragon
324 A St., South Boston, 617-338-8585
www.ming.com

CLINCH A MEAL
WITH THIS CHEF

The doyenne of Boston's culinary culture, James Beard Award-winning chef Barbara Lynch has built an empire of restaurants here in her hometown, and it's high time you experienced one. Whether your pocketbook is modest or weighted with gold, you've got options.

No. 9 Park

Sophisticated take on rustic French and Italian cuisine
Signature dish: prune-stuffed gnocchi

9 Park St., Boston, 617-742-9991
www.no9park.com

B&G Oysters

Modern classic oyster bar
Signature dish: Lobster roll

550 Tremont St., Boston, 617-423-0550
www.bandgoysters.com

The Butcher Shop

Wine bar with focus on charcuterie
Signature dish: House-made pâté

552 Tremont St., Boston, 617-423-4800
www.thebutchershopboston.com

Sportello

Chic diner with counter service and Italian dishes
Signature dish: Tagliatelle Bolognese

348 Congress St., Boston, 617-737-1234
www.sportelloboston.com

Drink

Craft cocktail bar
Signature dish: On-the-spot mixology

348 Congress St., Boston, 617-695-1806
www.drinkfortpoint.com

Menton

Fine dining, multi-course tasting menu only
Signature dish: Butter soup

354 Congress St., Boston, 617-737-0099
www.mentonboston.com

GO FOR GOLD
AT GRILL 23

I'll just come out and say it: Grill 23 has the best steaks I've ever eaten. Ever. And I've eaten many steaks. Your mission at this thirty-year-old, mod-magnificent dining room is to order the hundred-day-aged prime rib eye, a specialty of the house. I could go into the fact that Grill 23 uses Freisian steer that's hormone- and antibiotic-free, but let's jump right to the sensual details. Can you imagine it? Eighteen ounces of slightly charred meat cascading across your taste buds that is so juicy that you can dredge your sea-salted potato tots through what remains pooling on your plate. This rib eye is rich in flavor and in price ($54 a pop), but your money is well spent, especially when you pair it with a glass of Sangiovese.

161 Berkeley St., Boston, 617-542-2255
www.grill23.com

MANGIA, MANGIA
AT RINO'S

The bedazzled hostess at Rino's magically appears to seat you after you have waited for and hour-and-a-half and you're ready to hit the road for the nearest Taco Bell. Starving doesn't even cover how you're feeling. But wait a minute more and skip the salad in order to dive straight into the appetizers, portions of which are massive. This is some of the best Italian food I've ever had. Tennis-ball-sized arancini with plum tomato sauce and polenta cakes with sauteed wild mushrooms are two among many. The food just keeps coming, with plates of ravioli, chicken parmesan, veal saltimbocca, and fresh pasta—all made in-house. You wouldn't think a residential section of Eastie would yield such a gourmet feast.

258 Saratoga St., East Boston, 617-567-7412
www.rinosplacc.com

EAT ITALIAN
IN THE NORTH END

Out-of-towners call it "Boston's Little Italy," but to locals, Boston's Italian-American enclave is, simply, the North End. Why should you go here? To eat, of course! More than one hundred restaurants across the neighborhood, which is only about a third of a square mile in size, make it a hot dining destination, featuring absolutely delicious culinary traditions from all over *Lo Stivale*. Since it's impossible to pick one establishment to win the coveted title of The Best Restaurant, herewith I'm recommending my personal faves:

The Daily Catch
A chalkboard menu, twenty seats, and sizzling seafood served in the pan, make for long lines here, despite the cash-only policy. Order anything with calamari, particularly the house-made 'black' pasta.

323 Hanover St., Boston, 617-523-8567
www.thedailycatch.com

La Summa
Homey and off the beaten path, this no-fuss place is also the only North End restaurant still owned by a family that lives in the North End. The signature dish is house-made pappardelle e melanzane.

30 Fleet St., Boston, 617-523-9503
www.lasumma.com

Lucia

Prepare to navigate Hanover Street's throngs to reach this restaurant, deep in the heart of the North End. Dishes hail from all over Italy; I like the veal saltimbocca.

415 Hanover St., Boston, 617-367-2353
www.luciaboston.com

Mamma Maria

Fine rustic-style meals are served in small, elegant rooms within a North Square row house. The menu changes frequently, but the Tuscan braised rabbit is a staple.

3 North Square, Boston, 617-523-0077
www.mammamaria.com

Taranta

José Duarte's unique Hanover Street spot is not your average spaghetti joint. Southern Italy meets the chef's native Peru as entrees feature influences from the two continents.

210 Hanover St., Boston, 617-720-0052
www.tarantarist.com

Trattoria di Monica

With less than ten tables, this restaurant serves up a cozy vibe with candlelight and excellent food. All pasta is handmade on site, so you really can't go wrong.

67 Prince St., Boston, 617-720-5472
www.monicasboston.com

Caffe Paradiso

Park it at a cafe table for two and relax at this family-owned European-style cafe that serves Italian sweets, gelato, coffee drinks, apéritifs, and digestifs. It's a bit dark inside, even during the day, but large front windows open onto Hanover Street.

255 Hanover St., Boston, 617-742-1768
www.caffeparadiso.com

STAND IN LINE
FOR A SLICE

If your watch (oh, let's be real—your iPhone) reads 11:30 a.m. or later, you'll have to stand in line to score a table or a bar seat at Regina Pizzeria. But the wait is totally worth it for a piping hot pie fired in the landmark's signature brick oven. The compact North End location, decorated with neon beer signs, is the 1926 original of the small local chain that pops up at area shopping centers and transportation hubs. Purists will enjoy the original North End pie laced with light, herby tomato sauce and cheese, but more adventurous diners can dress it up with toppings like roasted eggplant, hot cherry peppers, or the house sausage. The kitchen makes the crust, stretched thin, from an eighty-year-old recipe.

11 1/2 Thacher St., Boston, 617-227-0765
www.reginapizzeria.com

SLURP THIS
CUPPA CHOWDER

If you're not a native of the New England region, chances are you've never had fish as fresh as that served at Boston restaurants, most of which source their catch daily from local fishers. While I can recommend a number of places for incredible seafood meals, the kingpin of them all, Legal Sea Foods, earned a reputation in the 1950s for quality and has since built an empire from Massachusetts to Georgia. Bet you didn't know that POTUS is a fan—Legal's clam chowder has been served at every presidential Inauguration since Reagan was in office. Might be worth trying a cup at one of the fifteen locations across Boston, Cambridge, and Somerville. Just sayin'. . .

255 State St., Boston, 617-742-5300
www.legalseafoods.com

GET HAPPY
AT MASA'S BAR

"Happy Hour" by traditional drink-special standards is illegal in Massachusetts and has been since the '80s, but this hasn't stopped local watering holes from bringing in after-work crowds with bar-only food specials. In my humble opinion, Masa, a longstanding Southwestern restaurant in the South End, serves up the greatest deal in town with its all-the-time dollar tapas that sink as low as fifty cents Sunday through Thursday from 5 p.m. until 7 p.m. Order 'em singly or by the board of ten available daily bites. Queso fundido empanada, duck confit on polenta cake, or chili almond-stuffed date wrapped in bacon . . . Wash it down with the house margarita. Best Meal Deal Ever!

439 Tremont St., Boston, 617-338-8884
www.masarestaurant.com

ORDER A SIDE OF JAZZ
WITH YOUR FOOD

After chancing upon this basement-level Harvard Square hideaway that happens to be wildly popular with Cantabrigians, prepare to spend the evening sipping exclusive small-batch wines on tap while listening to maybe the smoothest set you've heard live, ever. People flock here because its atmosphere is way out of the norm, with oversized beaded chandeliers and groovy painted wall murals, champagne by the glass-and-a-half, and dishes with names like Earth Bowl and Hippie Salad. Then there's the music which enhances rather than overwhelms the mood with blends of funk, percussion, electric soul, and dinner-style jazz, played by artists ranging from locals to Grammy Award winners.

13 Brattle St., Cambridge, 617-499-0001
www.beathotel.com

SNIFF YOUR DRINK
AT CAFÉ ARTSCIENCE

The punch at the bar at Café ArtScience in Kendall Square is not of the fruit-and-sherbet variety. Punch, then, is what you do to the rose-scented, bitters-laced sugar tulle disk that seals the snifter glass of the Le Whaf cocktail you just ordered. Cracking through it allows you to inhale the vaporized alcohol that's swirling around inside. That's right. You're sniffing booze. What's this, you say? It's an innovative and sensorial approach to mixology cooked up by biomedical engineer, inventor, and mad scientist David Edwards especially for this restaurant he opened near campus at MIT, and you need to try it out. Inhaling the vapors is meant to cleanse your palate, preparing it for the aforementioned Le Whaf. Once you've inhaled, pour your selected libation over flavored ice cubes and enjoy the expertly mixed real thing.

650 East Kendall St., Cambridge, 857-999-2193
www.cafeartscience.com

TAP INTO
BOSTON'S ORIGINAL BEER BAR

Before craft beer was a "thing," Sunset Grill & Tap was pouring it by the pint . . . like, way back in the 1980s. At first glance, you might describe this Allston bar as no-frills, but one look at its menu of hoppy options and you can see that there clearly are frills: namely, 113 beers on tap and nearly 400 microbrews and imports, including Barleywine, barrel-aged, lambics and wee-heavys, milk stouts, meads and witbier. Order by pint, pitcher, yard, or flight of five-ounce pours. If you still think none of these brews have the touch, PBR is five bucks a can.

130 Brighton Ave., Boston, 617-254-1331
www.allstonsfinest.com

TOAST CRAFT COCKTAILS
BY TOP TENDERS

Drink

By 4:45 p.m. on a Wednesday afternoon, this aptly titled Fort Point hangout is buzzing with after-work imbibers at its angular, wooden bar. At first glance, this setting may appear plain Jane, but that's only because proprietor Barbara Lynch wants you to focus on what you're drinking. As you should. There's no cocktail menu to speak of; instead, just tell the bartender what spirits and flavors you like, and he or she will conjure something on the spot. Don't even consider ordering an Apple-tini.

348 Congress St., Boston, 617-695-1806
www.drinkfortpoint.com

The Hawthorne

Legendary Boston mixologist Jackson Cannon is the proprietor of this sophisticated cocktail bar that serves up a Manhattan and a seasonal sherry cobbler with equal finesse. It's a place where bartenders are well versed in the history of spirits, know which mix well together, and can do the classics with or without a modern twist. Keep your eyes open, because the entrance is a little hard to find, but when you do, feel the living room lounge vibe, and save me a spot on the couch!

500A Commonwealth Ave., Boston, 617-532-9150
www.thehawthornebar.com

Wink & Nod

A gentlemanly doorman greets you at this den of cocktail craftsmanship, where funk music and near darkness sets a cooler-than-most tone. Your eyes will adjust fairly quickly, and when they do you'll behold a chandelier-lit modern speakeasy without the ironic pretension. Bourbon, scotch, vodka, and gin play starring roles on the menu of cocktails served up, down, or long, and made entirely from scratch, including house-concocted ingredients like ginger beer, fruit cordials, and bitters. A duo of tiki drinks packs such a punch that you're only allowed to order one.

3 Appleton St., Boston, 617-482-0117
www.winkandnod.com

EAT, DRINK, PEE
WITHOUT MISSING AN INNING

Follow the red neon arrow into The Bleacher Bar on Lansdowne Street for the cheapest ticket to the day's Boston Red Sox home game. How cheap? Free, aside from the cost of the beers and signature deli-style sandwiches you'll be consuming—tastier and far less expensive than the Fenway frank you'd be munching inside the ballpark. This modern watering hole tucks under Fenway Park's left-field bleacher seats and boasts a giant glass garage-door-style window that shows off a field-level view of all the action. What's more, there's no need to wait for the end of an inning to use the facilities for fear of missing Big Papi hit a home run—a window above the urinals in the men's room also offers unobstructed views. Ladies, you're out of luck on this one.

82A Lansdowne St., Boston, 617-262-2424
www.bleacherbarboston.com

SCREAM FOR ICE CREAM
AT CHRISTINA'S

There's a reason ice cream is one of the signature desserts of a New England summer. It's cool on the palate when the weather is oh-so-sweaty, and it's just darn good. Among the pack of local creameries, Christina's stands out as one of the best. Better yet, you don't have to go to Vermont to taste it. Every day more than forty creamy, tempting, handmade flavors stock the cases of this modest Inman Square landmark. Basics like chocolate and vanilla are always available, but encourage your taste buds to walk on the wild side with Mexican chocolate, malted vanilla, burnt sugar, fresh rose, adzuki bean, or dandelion burdock. Then take a seat on one of a few church pews and thank the heavens for this cup of divine stuff.

1255 Cambridge St., Cambridge, 617-492-7021
www.christinasicecream.com

TEA OFF
IN THIS TOWN

Time for a Boston tea party! This stuff of British tradition earned eternal notoriety in the New World when Samuel Adams and friends dumped it into Boston Harbor in 1773. Since those days are long gone and we again love to love the Brits, celebrate their heritage and ours with a formal afternoon tea.

The Reserve at the Langham

Special teas poured into custom-made Wedgwood china and locally inspired nibbles like house-smoked salmon and crème fraîche on Boston brown bread are served daily.

250 Franklin St., Boston, 617-451-1900 ext 8755
www.langhamhotels.com

Boston Public Library

Offered Wednesday through Friday, the BPL's Courtyard Restaurant pairs premium loose-leaf tea and three tiers of bite-sized snacks with views of an open-air courtyard garden.

230 Dartmouth St., Boston, 617-859-2251
www.thecateredaffair.com/bpl/courtyard

Rowes Wharf Sea Grille

Sweeping views of Boston Harbor enhance this daily offering. Savor tea blends and treats that reflect the season then spice up the afternoon with a boozy Tea-Tail.

70 Rowes Wharf, Boston, 617-856-7744
www.roweswharfseagrille.com

The Lounge at Taj

This historic Back Bay hotel hosts a luxurious weekend tea experience: pastries, petits fours, finger sandwiches, and canapés, with champagne accomp animent.

15 Arlington St., Boston, 617-598-5255
www.tajhotels.com

L'Espalier

Frank McClelland's fine French restaurant puts a fun spin on tradition with exclusive tea blends and servings whimsically named "Little Red Riding Hood's Basket."

774 Boylston St., Boston, 617-262-3023
www.lespalier.com

MUSIC AND ENTERTAINMENT

FALL IN LOVE
WITH A (NUTCRACKER) PRINCE

Icons of Christmas in America: Santa, Frosty, Rudolph, Ralphie, Irving Berlin, the Grinch, *The Nutcracker*. It's the last icon that we're talking about here, because this wildly popular, magical ballet danced by the Snow King, the Sugar Plum Fairy, Clara, and its titular character is a signature of Boston Ballet's season. The story goes something like this: Germany, 1820s. A wealthy family throws a party on Christmas Eve, at which toys come to life and a girl falls in love with her prince. Although Boston Ballet has been presenting the enchanting tale annually since 1965, Artistic Director Mikko Nissinen choreographed an entirely new version of *The Nutcracker* in 2012 which dazzles at the Opera House with jewel-encrusted costumes, snow flurries, a mouse army, and Arabian dancers. The legacy of the 1892 score by Tchaikovsky in this country extends back to the mid-20th century. Notably, the San Francisco Ballet featured the American premier of *Nutcracker* in 1944; today, Helgi Tomasson's 2004 re-envisioning runs for two weeks in December. And New York City Ballet presents George Balanchine's *Nutcracker* choreographed by the company's famous founder in 1954. Both New York's and Boston's ballet companies perform it from Thanksgiving until the very start of the new year. It is true—you can see *The Nutcracker* performed in almost every U.S. city, but Boston's dreamy rendering is exceptional, even critically acclaimed by the *The New York Times*.

Performances typically run Thanksgiving through New Year's Day.

Boston Opera House, 539 Washington St., Boston, 617-695-6955
www.bostonballet.org

HEAR HAYDN
AS HAYDN DID

Handel, Mozart, Mendelssohn, Vivaldi. These names—so well known yet so far removed from our own here-and-now. It's crazy to imagine that the period-instrument orchestra and chorus Handel and Haydn Society has been around long enough to have premiered some of these composers' works in America. But indeed it has, celebrating its bicentennial in 2015. Don't know what "period-instrument orchestra and chorus" means? It indicates that today's musicians recreate what the piece would have sounded like during the era in which it was written by using instruments and techniques from way back then. The result leads to a richness of sound and a more fanciful interpretation, played in a setting iconic in its own right—Boston's Symphony Hall.

Season typically runs October through May.

617-266-3605
www.handelandhaydn.org

FIND THIS HALL
ALIVE WITH MUSIC

The incredible acoustics at Symphony Hall allow fans of classical music to really jam when the world-class Boston Symphony Orchestra is in the house. This Big 5 ensemble is among the best in the world. Latvian-born BSO Music Director Andris Nelsons conducts concerts and operas with finesse while a roster of special guest musicians, singers, and conductors reads like a Who's Who of today's most elite performers. If you're not in the know about the classical genre but find yourself on the receiving end of a ticket, go anyway. You might just change your tune.

Season is October through April.

Symphony Hall, 301 Massachusetts Ave., Boston, 617-266-1492
www.bso.org

TIP: Attend one of the BSO's open rehearsals instead of an evening performance for a fraction of the price; usually $18-30.

GET DOWN
AT THE DONKEY SHOW

At this point, Boston's buttoned-up arts patrons have grown accustomed to Diane Paulus's risk-taking approach to theater. After all, since she grabbed the reins at American Repertory Theater as Artistic Director in 2009, she's moved two of her A.R.T. productions—*Pippin* and the Gershwins' *Porgy and Bess*—to Broadway, directed Cirque du Soleil's *Amaluna*, and won a Tony Award. So she must be doing something right. What you must do on this list of 100 things is experience the spectacle that marked her entree into Boston: the *Donkey Show*, a cheeky, disco-licious fantasy that she created with her husband, Randy Weiner. Not for the faint-hearted, this bare-chested, confetti-dusted dance party is Paulus's shakeup of Shakespeare's *A Midsummer Night's Dream*, and it remains one of local nightlife's hottest attractions, now six years and 500-plus performances deep. Stare up at the spinning mirror ball and get ready to boogie.

Performances run Saturday evenings.

Oberon, 2 Arrow St., Cambridge, 617-547-8300
www.americanrepertorytheater.org

FIND THE SPOTLIGHT
AT HUNTINGTON THEATRE COMPANY

Local theater goers know that artistic director Peter DuBois puts together season after season of groundbreaking plays for Huntington Theatre Company. In general, expect polished new works from contemporary playwrights like Ronan Noone and Christopher Durang mixed with classics by Chekhov, Wilder and, occasionally, the Bard himself. At the top of its game among regional theaters, the Huntington also attracts an experienced cast. Kate Burton and Campbell Scott are regular fixtures. Billy Porter, Mary Zimmerman, and Nick Offerman have worked magic here in the last few years. What are you waiting for? Go see a show already!

Performances run September through May.

617-266-0800
www.huntingtontheatre.org

WAVE A FLAG
ON THE FOURTH WITH THE BOSTON POPS

Philharmonic performance meets rock concert meets patriotic jamboree beneath red, white, and blue lights—that's what rolls onto the Hatch Shell stage on July 4th every summer when the Boston Pops orchestra hosts its annual national birthday bash. Led by the always-peppy Keith Lockhart and backed by sunset views of the Charles River, this musical evening doesn't discriminate on its set list, pivoting fluidly from John Williams's *Star Wars* score to George Cohan's *I'm a Yankee Doodle Dandy* to Tchaikovsky's dramatic *1812 Overture*. The show is free but attracts enormous crowds. It also launches one of the biggest fireworks displays of the year.

July 3-4

DCR Hatch Memorial Shell, Storrow Drive
www.bostonpops.org

FEEL THE GOOD VIBRATIONS
[TOP SMALL MUSIC CLUBS]

For when you're looking for a beer, an intimate show, seats within a stone's throw of the stage, and little-to-zero cover:

Lizard Lounge
While rock and roots are a focus of this basement club, eclectic acts run the gamut from groove to opera. Solidly into its teen years, the popular Sunday night Poetry Jam & Slam features spoken word performances backed by the Jeff Robinson Trio.

1667 Massachusetts Ave., Cambridge, 617-547-0759
www.lizardloungeclub.com

The Plough & Stars
Halfway between Harvard and Central Squares, this Irish bar-gastropub hosts some of the best live performers working the 02139 zip code.

912 Massachusetts Ave., Cambridge, 617-576-0032
www.ploughandstars.com

Wally's Cafe
Guaranteed there's someone jamming at Wally's tonight—this place is open 365 days a year. It debuted back in 1947 during the big band era, but these days the teeny, historic club promotes a mix of Berklee students and jazz-funk pros.

427 Massachusetts Ave., Boston, 617-424-1408
www.wallyscafe.com

FEEL THE GOOD VIBRATIONS
[TOP MEDIUM-SIZED MUSIC CLUBS]

Tickets cost a little bit more, but talent is professional and often Grammy Award-winning. Bonus: each of these three also serves dinner with the show:

Club Passim
Joan Baez got her start here, and Dylan played, too. Today, up-and-coming singer-songwriters rule the stage, and Lori McKenna is a mainstay.

47 Palmer St., Cambridge, 617-492-7679
www.clubpassim.org

Johnny D's
Hear truly awesome blues, soul, funk, roots, rock, and acts from across the world. The weekly Sunday afternoon open mic Blues Jam is legendary.

17 Holland St., Somerville, 617-776-2004
www.johnnyds.com

Scullers Jazz Club
On any given night, masters like Donal Fox, Poncho Sanchez, or Michael Bublé could be playing the sweet sounds of all styles of contemporary jazz, from improv to Latin.

400 Soldiers Field Road, Boston, 866-777-8932
www.scullersjazz.com

FIND THE CRAIC
IN SOUTHIE

Bostonians play a holiday doubleheader every March 17, celebrating both St. Patrick's Day and Evacuation Day with one grand event—the St. Patrick's Day Parade. Let me say that if you loathe crowds, this event is not for you, but those who don't mind hanging with more than half-a-million spectators should attend at least once this lifetime. Fife and drum players, marching bands, members of the armed forces, police, and politicians march through South Boston to honor the neighborhood's vibrant Irish heritage, as well as the expulsion of the British regulars from Dorchester Heights, ending the Siege of Boston in 1776. People-watching ranges from adorable Irish kids in glittery green hats to proud war veterans to twenty-somethings in the midst of a Sunday afternoon "pahtee."

Sunday closest to March 17

Start: Broadway Station, South Boston
Finish: Andrew Square, South Boston
844-478-7287
www.southbostonparade.org

RING IN THE NEW YEAR
AT FIRST NIGHT BOSTON

What does eleven hours of arts or entertainment cost in Boston on New Year's Eve? You'll have to pony up ten bucks for an all-access button to the outdoor festival First Night Boston, its 200 indoor events and performances included. Take it from this native New Englander: dress warmly rather than fashionably. Then you can fully experience the country's largest and longest-running New Year's Eve arts festival without worrying about whether your frostbitten fingers are going to turn black and fall off. Hosted by the City of Boston, First Night is alcohol-free and family-friendly, so don't be afraid to throw caution to the wind and bring the kids. Parties, parades, live music and dance, ice sculpting, skating, and two—count 'em, two—fireworks displays give hearty welcome to the upcoming year.

December 31

www.firstnightboston.org

CATCH A FLICK
[SILENTS TO THE AVANT-GARDE]

Calling all cinephiles: this is your gig. Harvard Film Archive screens movies you never thought you'd see on the big screen and often invites the directors to speak about them in person, like American screenwriter and director Elaine May or internationally acclaimed Filipino filmmaker Lav Diaz. HFA runs monthly series and retrospectives, shows experimental works, and explores the cinema culture of other countries. An evening here is a bargain at nine bucks—less than it costs to see Hollywood's latest blockbuster and for a far richer experience.

Carpenter Center, 24 Quincy St., Cambridge, 617-495-4700
hcl.harvard.edu/hfa

STAND UP FOR COMEDY
AT THE STUDIO

Don't for a minute assume that the scorpion bowls served at this longtime Harvard Square comedy club are meant to put more of a punch in the punch lines of local comics working the stage. Otherwise, would Steven Wright be a regular in the audience? I think not. This bare-bones third-floor space always hosts a smorgasbord of talent, from students of sketch comedy at Emerson College to a comedy-magic show hybrid. My favorite to catch is the signature weekly *Big Saturday Night Show* where newbies and comics you may have seen on Conan riff with equal grandeur. Seriously, Wright, Louis C.K., and Eugene Mirman, among others, have been known to drop in.

1238 Massachusetts Ave., Cambridge, 617-661-6507
www.thecomedystudio.com

THEN SKETCH IT OUT
AT IMPROV ASYLUM

If you ever call for tickets to a local show ahead of time, do so now. This homegrown comedy endeavor is as hilarious as it gets, and consequently, seats are harder to come by than ice pops in hell. Talking in analogies, I'd say Improv Asylum is to Boston as Second City is to Chicago. Performers mix it up with sketch comedy and say-it-as-you-think-it improv, so no one show is ever exactly like another. Plus, the club is located in the North End among hordes of Italian restaurants (see pages 30 and 31), which means you and your gal or your buddies can make a whole delicious night of it.

216 Hanover St., Boston, 617-263-6887
www.improvasylum.com

SPORTS AND RECREATION

ROOT FOR THE RED SOX
AT FENWAY PARK

If it's baseball season, one must go see a Red Sox game at Fenway Park. No seat is far from the action at this intimate 1912 stadium that beats out Chicago's Wrigley Field by two years for the title of oldest in the Major Leagues. Spectators range from pink hats to purists (old-timers who can detail games that happened decades into the past). But for all who attend, there's nothing quite like sitting amid the energized throngs of Red Sox Nation, alternately cheering and groaning as Fenway's quirky features stymie star players who have to hit around the Green Monster or Pesky's Pole. The Red Sox have made upgrades to the park in recent years but have been careful to carry on time-honored traditions. A lucky few fans can even sit in original wood grandstand seats and imagine what they've witnessed: Ted Williams at bat, the Babe on the mound, Big Papi, Jim Rice, Cy Young, Bobby Doerr, Pedro Martinez, Carl Yastrzemski. Before the first at-bat, there is time to mill about on Yawkey Way with fellow game goers, a sausage and a beer in hand. For as little as $10 per ticket, there's no excuse to miss this.

Season is April through October.

4 Yawkey Way, Boston, 877-RedSox-9
www.redsox.com

OR JUST HAUNT
BASEBALL'S OLDEST BALLPARK

But it doesn't have to be baseball season to gain access to America's oldest and most revered ballpark. Heck, you don't even have to be a baseball fan to appreciate the 103 years of history uncovered in its hallowed tunnels and underbelly. Hour-long guided Fenway Park Tours visit the press box, the Monster Seats, the grandstand, and more. Along the way, learn that the Boston Red Sox was originally named the Americans from 1903 to 1907 and that the Sox was the first team to win the first World Series ever played—while you examine the actual championship trophy. See a display exhibit titled "Fenway and the Greatest Generation" which spotlights Sox players and their military service through items like Ted Williams's Marines aviator jacket. Find out which bricks of Fenway Park are original, and then sit in the oldest seats—literally—in Major League Baseball.

Gate D Ticket Booth, Yawkey Way at Van Ness Street, Boston
617-226-6666
www.redsox.com

SEE TOM TOSS THE BALL
AT THE RAZOR WHILE YOU STILL CAN

Football fan or not, before Tom Brady retires or you die, you've got to see New England's fabled QB toss the pigskin live at his home field, Gillette Stadium. He's pushing 40 after all, and well, that's getting old in the pro arena. At the completion of the 2014 season, Brady has led the Patriots to six Super Bowls, winning four of them. He's a three-time Super Bowl MVP and a two-time NFL MVP, he's thrown more than fifty touchdowns in a single season, and he's had three seasons where he's averaged more than 300 passing yards per game. Joe Montana who? Brady is the NFL's best QB ever (yeah, we said it).

Season is August through January.

Gillette Stadium, 1 Patriot Place, Foxboro, 508-543-1776
www.patriots.com

TIP

Gillette Stadium is about twenty miles from Boston, but it's easy to get there via the New England Patriots Football Trains, a special MBTA service that departs Boston a few hours before kickoff. $15. www.mbta.com

CATCH A GAME
AT THE 'GAHDEN' [HOCKEY]

Look out for the big bad Bruins. Boston's hometown NHL team cultivates an experience that the uninitiated need to be ready for. In the stands of the TD Garden, a rabid, lunch-pail fan base cheers for—and jeers at—players, hoping for another great 'Gahden' moment like Bobby Orr's goal in overtime during Game 4 of the 1970 Stanley Cup Final against the St. Louis Blues. The Bruins are one of the NHL's original six teams and one of the most storied franchises in North America. In 2011, the team won the Stanley Cup, and today it features seriously stellar players like Tuukka Rask, Patrice Bergeron, Zdeno Chára, and Milan Lucic. If you're easily offended, this one's not for you.

Season is October through April.

TD Garden, 100 Legends Way, Boston, 617-624-2327
www.bruins.nhl.com

TIP

Soak up the atmosphere with a beer before or after a game at Sully's (Sullivan's Tap), a dive bar across the street from the Garden and favorite hangout among local hockey enthusiasts.

CATCH A GAME
AT THE 'GAHDEN' [BASKETBALL]

Round two at the 'Gahden,' this time to see the Boston Celtics move the ball up and down the basketball court. The Celts have the most titles in NBA history with seventeen, and if you count championships as a measure of greatness, then former Celtics center Bill Russell is at the top of that list with eleven, earned from 1957 to 1969. Boston's team hit it big again in the 1980s, thanks to the Big Three (Larry Bird, Kevin McHale, and Robert Parrish) and most recently in 2008, thanks to the New Big Three (Paul Pierce, Kevin Garnett, and Ray Allen). These days, the team and the coach have completely changed over, and it's exciting to imagine what will happen next. So be there to witness it.

Season is October through April.

TD Garden, 100 Legends Way, Boston, 866-423-5849
www.nba.com/celtics

TIP

Here's your alternative to an out-of-control day at the mall on Black Friday: a Celtics-Bruins doubleheader, a ritual that takes place on the day after Thanksgiving.

CHEER ON
THE CRIMSON

Like any long-standing rivalry, the Harvard vs. Yale football game is worth seeing if for no other reason than being able to say that you went to the Harvard-Yale game. Played every other year at historic Harvard Stadium, which resembles a horseshoe-shaped Roman coliseum—and alternately at the Yale Bowl— The Game is a staunch tradition attended by students, alumni, and fans. Sight lines of the field are notably great, but do avoid sitting behind the stadium's columns which obstruct views for spectators in the uppermost sections. Don't miss the pre-game festivities. Anyone who has dough enough to send their kid to Harvard won't skimp on tailgating food. Friends and I once ended up next to a Harvard cheerleader's dad who owned a barbecue restaurant in Memphis and felt great about sharing his haul of tasty treats. Go Crimson!

November

65 N. Harvard St., Boston, 617-495-2211
www.gocrimson.com

HEAD TO THE CHARLES
FOR HEAD OF THE CHARLES

This annual rowing competition is a very big deal, internationally. The site you choose to take in two days of races determines your experience. On the Cambridge bank between Harvard and Central squares, there is a constant buzz of activity. If you don't mind a crowd, this is a great spot for spreading a blanket because views of rowers as they turn a bend in the river and glide beneath the Weeks Footbridge are spectacular. Thanks to loads of food vendors, the aromas of sausages, barbecued meat, and charcoaled burgers waft through the air, enticing passersby to fill their bellies. It's all very collegiate in this area, as the brick facades of Harvard University River Houses abut Memorial Drive and crowds of spectators dress in Crimson hats and windbreakers. Further upstream near the finish line and the Regatta's headquarters at Cambridge Boating Club, the atmosphere is more mellow. Fans move aside bushes and other riverbank scrub to sit in small groups and cheer on the athletes.

Third weekend in October

www.hocr.org

JOSTLE FOR A SPOT
AT THE BOSTON MARATHON FINISH LINE

The Boston Marathon was a huge deal even before the tragic 2013 bombing at its finish line landed it in headlines across the world. Organized by the Boston Athletic Association, the prestigious race is part of the World Marathon Majors series, the planet's six largest and most renowned marathons. It celebrates 120 years in 2016 and is infamous for its deceptive route, which first-timers learn begins quick, easy, and angled downhill before it shackles runners with a series of brutal uphill climbs at Mile 20. Statistics aside, the real heart of the Boston Marathon is exhibited by the spectators who come to cheer on the athletes. The mood along Boylston Street near the finish swells with emotion as the crowd of onlookers roars all afternoon, cheering on and encouraging every numbered, sweat-wicking jersey that sails past. If you've been there before, well, you know what I'm talking about, and if you haven't, then go find out!

Third Monday of April

Start: Main Street, Hopkinton, Mass.
Finish: Boylston Street at Dartmouth Street, Boston
www.baa.org

SET YOUR SIGHTS
ON THE SEA

Pick up the Boston Harborwalk at Long Wharf and head south on foot. Although there is a serious lack of sand, you are actually skirting the city's shoreline. Well-marked with blue directional signs, this paved coastal stroll ventures through different neighborhoods and boasts bar-none water views that change with every step. Downtown, see fancy yachts at Rowes Wharf and stop for a lobster roll at James Hook (page 5). Next up: the site of the Boston Tea Party and the fourteenth floor observation deck at 470 Atlantic Ave. which offers aerial views of Fort Point Channel and the Greenway. Turn left at Northern Avenue to follow the Harborwalk into South Boston's Seaport District, along Fan Pier, past the Moakley Federal Courthouse and the Institute of Contemporary Art. This at-leisure tour winds around the World Trade Center, allowing your eyes a close-up gander at inner harbor boat traffic and the working fish pier. Be on your guard for kamikaze gulls and the roaring planes lifting off from Logan Airport.

www.bostonharborwalk.com

MAKE WAY
FOR YOUR DUCKLINGS...

If you're a parent and/or a Bostonian and you've never read Robert McCloskey's 1942 Caldecott Medal-winning children's book *Make Way for Ducklings*, then shame on you. Go pick up a copy and the kiddos—you're about to trace the mallard family's journey on foot and take in some sights while doing so. From the always-in-bloom Public Garden to the Swan Boats, the State House, well-to-do Louisburg Square, the Charles River Esplanade, Charles Street, and back over to the Garden, it's fun to read each page on location. The journey is not terribly long, but if the little ones are young, consider a stroller.

Public Garden, Beacon Street at Charles Street, 617-723-8144

TIP
I'll even tell you where to buy
McCloskey's book: Blackstone's
of Beacon Hill on Charles Street
always has it in stock.
Now you have no excuse.

... THEN QUACK
LIKE ONE

If you've been in town for more than an hour and it's not the middle of winter, you've likely noticed the brightly painted, odd-looking, and massive vehicles driving around the Back Bay. Say hello to Boston Duck Tours. These tour buses are actually replicas of World War II DUKW amphibious craft. BDT uses them to tool around on land and then coast into the Charles for a thirty-minute water ride. "Conducktors" (yuk, yuk) put a theatrical spin on guiding, acting out character personalities that are, in a word, wacky. What the history buff in me loves about BDT is that every time I take a tour, I learn something I didn't know about Boston's history, which is saying a lot since I've been writing about this place for fifteen years, and I grew up here.

March through November

Departs three locations: Huntington entrance of the Shops at Prudential Center, Museum of Science, and New England Aquarium, 617-267-3825
www.bostonducktours.com

SPEND THE NIGHT
ON BOSTON HARBOR, LITERALLY

Drop anchor at the *Liberty Star* the next time you come to town and spend the night rocking and rolling to the lapping waves of Boston Harbor. To be sure, this is no climate-controlled Marriott. But it's a gorgeous coastal schooner that's part of the Liberty Fleet of Tall Ships and a temporary bunk for up to six would-be sailors wanting to essentially camp out in downtown Boston. Cabins are basic and the head is shared, but unless you own a sailboat, how else could you say you got to sleep on one?

June through mid-September

Liberty Star docks at Central Wharf.
Liberty Fleet Office, 67 Long Wharf, Boston, 617-742-0333
www.libertyfleet.com

SEE BOSTON
FROM THE SKY

Boston might be a small city compared to U.S. heavyweights Chicago, New York, and LA, but it's got one of the prettiest and most diverse skylines, retaining many of its original eighteenth- and nineteenth-century buildings and unhampered by hordes of humongous buildings. Neighborhoods, bridges, ball parks, mountains, rivers, islands, the sea, it's all right here for your viewing pleasure.

Skywalk Observatory

Luckily for visitors, there's an elevator that zips up fifty stories to the top of Prudential Center, Boston's second-tallest building. The bird's-eye perspective here stretches into greater New England, as far as 100 miles. Closer by, peek down into Fenway Park, across the Charles River, and all around the Back Bay.

800 Boylston St., Boston, 617-859-0648

Bunker Hill Monument

The Charlestown obelisk and high point of the Freedom Trail commemorates the first major battle of the American Revolution--although technically it's misnamed--because all the action took place on Breeds Hill where the monument sits. It's an uphill slog to even reach the base, then another 221 feet to the top for a look back at Boston from across the harbor.

Monument Square, Charlestown, 617-242-5601

Washington Tower

Mount Auburn Cemetery in Cambridge is home to the Washington Tower. Climb ninety-six steps to the top for a panoramic view of the Boston skyline—one of the best, according to Ben Affleck who filmed scenes from *Gone Baby Gone* onsite.

580 Mount Auburn St., Cambridge, 617-547-7105

Rooftop Observation Deck at Independence Wharf

It's completely free to get into this little-known observatory in the Financial District. Bring a coat (unless it's summer) and identification (you'll need to show it to get in) for an unencumbered fourteenth-floor view of Fort Point Channel, the Seaport District, South Boston, and FiDi.

470 Atlantic Ave., Boston, 617-737-0974

OWN
THE EMERALD NECKLACE...

From the filling in of tidal flats to the leveling of hills, Boston's topography has undergone a complete transformation since William Blaxton grazed his cows here in 1628. This took centuries, of course. One of the major projects of the late nineteenth century comes courtesy of Frederick Law Olmsted, who created an interconnected system of six parks called the Emerald Necklace, essentially building green space where there had been none. Incidentally, the landscape architect and preservationist would go on to plan New York's Central Park and Niagara Reservation at Niagara Falls, among others. Today city dwellers are fortunate to be able to continue to enjoy his vision. Your task: make the most of it. Launch a rowboat at Jamaica Pond. Zigzag across the Back Bay Fens. Listen to live music at Olmsted Park. Walk it from its beginning at Franklin Park to its end at Boston Common; it's seven meandering, shaded miles.

Start: Boston Common, Boston
Finish: Franklin Park, Dorchester
www.emeraldnecklace.org

TIP

Major sites along, but not part of, the Emerald Necklace include the 275-acre Forest Hills Cemetery where Lucy Stone and Eugene O'Neill rest and Franklin Park Zoo with its animals from around the globe.

...AND TAKE EXTRA TIME
AT ARNOLD ARBORETUM

One of the singular gems of Olmsted's Emerald Necklace is the Arnold Arboretum, owned by Harvard University. Whether you like to study trees or not, you'll need at least an afternoon to amble across this park's 281 acres. Bussey Hill is a high point, literally, so ensnare a stick and use it to help hike the summit for a 360 degree view of Great Blue Hill and the Boston skyline. Then hide among the groves of juniper and spruce trees near Conifer Path, which make you want to live under one in a game of extreme fort building. In late spring, get a whiff of one of the country's most significant and fragrant lilac collections. Jump across bubbling brooks. Join a "tree mob." Seek out the oversized metal "dog tags" swinging from the branches on each of 15,000 trees, offering would-be horticulturists insight on species and native environment.

125 Arborway, Boston, 617-384-5209
arboretum.harvard.edu

PITCH A TENT
ON THE BOSTON HARBOR ISLANDS

Did you know there are almost three dozen tiny islands floating in Boston Harbor? Many Bostonians haven't caught on to this sweet little secret, even though collectively they've been recognized as a National Recreation Area by the National Park Service. The adventurous and seriously low-maintenance crowd can and should pitch a tent for a rustic overnight experience on one of the four islands that allow camping. This includes gathering your own firewood, no electricity, and a carry-on, carry-off policy. With luck you'd have composting toilets. On the flip side, I'd say you're pretty lucky to wander sand and shell beaches, pick wild berries, and otherwise explore these remote islands that centuries ago were home to forts, hospitals, and farmhouses.

Mid-June through Labor Day
Reservations must be made at 877-422-6762
www.reservamerica.com

Bumpkin, Lovells, Grape, and Peddocks islands
www.bostonharborislands.org

INVESTIGATE FORT WARREN
[YOU'LL NEED A FLASHLIGHT]

Georges Island, the hub of the Boston Harbor Islands National Recreation Area, typically flies under the radar of popular historical and recreational pursuits despite being one of the city's most valuable natural and cultural attractions. Upon its thirty-nine to fifty-three acres (the island's size changes according to the tide) sits Fort Warren, a federal bastion that was instrumental in Boston's coastal defense system from the Civil War era through World War II. Today the fort is listed on the Register as a National Historic Landmark, but locals in the know love it because it is one cool—and creepy—way to pass a day. The former Confederate prison's recessed granite chambers are minimally restored and lit narrowly by natural daylight, an effect that, when coupled with ostensible ghosts, keeps visitors glancing over their shoulders and wishing they had a flashlight. On a sunnier note, the central parade ground hosts activities including vintage baseball and lawn games authentic to the 1860s and is also a fabulous place for a picnic. Georges Island is the only one of thirty-four islands within the recreation area to feature a lunch counter. Surprisingly, the food, from crispy fish and chips to buttery grilled cheese, is excellent.

Ferries depart from Long Wharf North in Boston, and Hingham Ship Yard in Hingham, Mass., May through Columbus Day.

Boston Harbor Islands Pavilion, 191 Atlantic Ave., Boston, 617-223-8666
www.bostonharborislands.org

SPOT A SPOUT
ON A WHALE WATCH

Hop aboard a Boston Harbor Cruises catamaran and start scanning the horizon for puffs of white smoke—you're headed thirty miles off the coast of Boston to seriously prime territory for whale watching. Nutrient-rich feeding ground, Stellwagen Bank is easily one of the world's best locations for this water sport because it is on the whales' migratory route between Canada and the Caribbean. New England Aquarium naturalists educate passengers on what to look for during this three-hour sail, like unusual splashing or dorsal fins at the surface. The time of season determines what kinds of marine animals and mammals you are likely to see. Humpback whales show off tricks while they feed, like creating bubble nets and occasionally fully breaching the surface with all the grace of Nadia Comăneci. Minke whales and finback whales are fairly common sights, as are Atlantic white-sided dolphins and ocean sunfish, a fish that can weigh up to a ton and lays on its side at the surface for warmth. And, well, if you don't see a single thing while you're out on the water, New England Aquarium and Boston Harbor Cruises give you a free ticket for a future ride.

May through October

Central Wharf, Boston, 877-733-9425
www.bostonharborcruises.com

DAY TRIP
TO P-TOWN

Beat it out of town for a whole day and experience the antithesis of this big, bad city. All the way on the tip of Cape Cod, Provincetown is a rural, rugged curl of sand dunes, sea grass, and a thriving LGBT community. The Pilgrims landed here before Plymouth Rock and then passed it up, but the artist and writer types of later centuries did not, giving us hugely talented residents like Jackson Pollock and Norman Mailer. Tourist shops and restaurants convene on Commercial Street. Definitely spend a couple hours at Race Point Beach on the Cape Cod National Seashore. Ferries from Boston cruise to Provincetown in a quick ninety minutes from mid-May through mid-October. By car, it would take you an hour longer, best case scenario. But if you've got money to burn, there are quick flights via Cape Air.

Boston Harbor Cruises
Long Wharf, Boston, 617-227-4321
www.bostonharborcruises.com

Bay State Cruise Company
World Trade Center Pier, Boston, 617-748-1428
www.baystatecruisecompany.com

Cape Air
Logan Airport, Boston, 800-227-3247
www.capeair.com

PARK IT
AT THE ROSE KENNEDY GREENWAY

Have you conquered the Esplanade's jogging paths and strolled through the Common and the Public Garden enough to consider yourself a veteran of downtown Boston's green spaces? If you haven't trekked here since late 2008, then you haven't been to our newest park which snakes through the Financial District and now occupies real estate that was formerly known as Interstate 93. Oh, the things to do at the Rose Kennedy Greenway! To satiate your shopping habit, there are two different farmers' markets during the week and an awesome artisan fair every Saturday from May until mid-October. Kids go berserk for the Greenway Carousel, an artist-designed and custom-built merry-go-round that features squirrels, lobsters, and even a sea serpent gondola for riding. There's live music, tribes of food trucks, and edible herb gardens. When summer really sets in, the Greenway boasts a whopping seven fountains for splashing and cooling off. So bring your swimsuit!

www.rosekennedygreenway.org

BOSTON CHILDREN'S MUSEUM

RECAPTURE YOUR YOUTH
AT THE CHILDREN'S MUSEUM

The youngsters will crown you a hero after taking them to the Boston Children's Museum, a place that has all the stuff of childhood dreams—except maybe unicorns. Rainbows, bubbles, tunnels, bobcats—they're all here. Exhibits are interactive and include "Construction Zone" for building larger structures tongue-and-groove style and "Arthur & Friends" where Elwood City comes alive at sites like Arthur's backyard and Mr. Ratburn's classroom. The Japanese House replicates an actual one-hundred-year-old domestic dwelling in Kyoto and is a shoe-free zone that kids can explore. But before all that, they can go wild clambering up the New Balance climb inside the museum lobby, a series of net platforms built three stories high, right up to the ceiling. Look out below!

308 Congress St., Boston, 617-426-6500
www.bostonchildrensmuseum.org

CONNECT
WITH THE HUMAN BODY

Ever wanted to reach right inside someone's gut for a closer look at their kidneys or large intestine (for scientific pursuits, of course, not Hannibal Lecter-style)? You're in luck! The torso coffee table within Museum of Science's Hall of Human Life lets you do just that, pulling out and rearranging the body's different vital organs in this giant 3-D puzzle. If you and the family really get into it, venture over to the Exploration Hub where volunteers occasionally dissect a real sheep's heart or a fetal pig and also show off the human ear they're growing. Health and disease, genetics and environment take the driver's seat. Make it personal by snagging an ID bracelet tagged with a serial number which you can use at fifteen different Link Stations. Each interactive station puts you through a test or activity, determines your results, and compares it with the live statistics of other museum goers.

After you've exhausted your efforts as a biologist-in-training, take a walk around the rest of the Museum. Overload your senses at the 4-D Theater, stand inside the Butterfly Garden where the winged creatures flutter freely around, and hold onto your hat during a lightening show in the Theater of Electricity.

1 Science Park, Boston, 617-723-2500

www.mos.org

TIP

For less than the cost of a regular movie theater ticket, you can catch a flick on the Museum's five-story, tall-domed IMAX screen. The visual odyssey is, in a word, intense.

LIVE THE FUTURE
AT MIT MUSEUM

Artificial intelligence? It's not so much a thing of the future at MIT Museum, where fans of Disney Pixar's *WALL-E* film go wild for Kismet, RoboTuna, and other "smart" robots invented at the super-techy university. This museum is small, but it tackles some hefty subject matter in a way that's easy for visitors to grasp. Gestural engineering (the art of kinetics), photography (Edwin Land founded Polaroid at MIT), and holography—reach right out and touch HRH Queen Elizabeth II's wrinkles in 3-D.

265 Massachusetts Ave., Cambridge, 617-253-5927
web.mit.edu/museum

TIP

The museum's gift shop yields cool gadgets like edible chemistry kits, lemon-powered clocks, and amoeba jigsaw puzzles. It's a worthy spot for the kids to spend their allowance money.

TAKE THE PLUNGE
WITH THE L STREET BROWNIES

One, two, three, GO. There's no taking it slow, dipping in a toe at a time. You do that, and you'll never complete this bucket-list task, which is to plunge into the icy waters of Pleasure Bay on New Year's Day, when temps average thirty degrees Fahrenheit. You may be reading this and thinking, "People are crazy, man." Well, yes; but, the L Street Brownies' annual Polar Plunge is more than a hundred years of dedicated crazy. Locals slip into their swimsuits for the dive of a lifetime, and you should, too. Just for the chilly thrill of it. Plus, if this doesn't cure a NYE hangover, what will?

L Street Bathhouse and Beach, 1663 Columbia Road, South Boston
617-635-5104
www.lstreetcurley.com

PAINT WITH SEALS
[BECAUSE, WHY NOT?]

Want to pet sting rays, coax penguins into chirping, and watch a massive sea turtle named Myrtle swim right in front of your face? Heck yeah! Spending a day at the New England Aquarium is always a valid reason for calling in sick, at least in my book, and I'll tell you why: the wondrous four-story Giant Ocean Tank, around which all other exhibits are placed, transforms you into miniature size, especially with its couple thousand fish and sharks circling inside. The Shark and Ray touch tank is ahh-mazing, in a word, and I find that children always get more out of an experience when it's tangible. Which leads me to a little-known NEAq program—Animal Encounters. On these, participants get to interact with real marine mammals and their trainers. "Paint with Seals" even has you assisting one of the friendly harbor seals as he uses paintbrushes fit with special grips to swipe paint all over a canvas. If you're sweet, you might get a kiss, and what's more, you get to take the painting home.

Central Wharf, Boston, 617-973-5200
www.neaq.org

CULTURE AND HISTORY

GLIDE
ON A GIANT SWAN

With its lazy walking paths and vast array of flowering beds, the Public Garden is a traffic-free escape from the twenty-first-century. In the 1830s, the city cordoned off part of the Boston Common, transforming it into a botanical garden. Perhaps its most endearing charm is the historic Swan Boats that have been gliding atop the shimmering green waters of its sun-dappled lagoon since the Victorian Era. The graceful pleasure boats offer a peddle-powered ride beneath rustling weeping willows. Passengers can wave to park-goers as they sail beneath a stone and steel suspension bridge (a la San Fran's iconic Golden Gate Bridge) built in 1867 and presumed to be the world's smallest. For preserving this carefree diversion, we can thank the Paget family which founded the avian-themed recreational pursuit back in 1877 and still operates it today.

Mid-April through mid-September

Public Garden, Charles Street South, Boston, 617-522-1966
www.swanboats.com

EMBRACE
THE MOTHER CHURCH

You would think that the eighth largest organ in the world would be a visit-worthy attraction on its own, but Boston's First Church of Christ, Scientist, a.k.a. the Mother Church, has so much more going on. Architecturally speaking, the unique combination of Romanesque, Byzantine, and Renaissance styles of the church building itself is absolutely gorgeous. There's no cost to further explore inside on thirty-minute guided tours.

210 Massachusetts Ave., Boston, 617-450-3790
www.christianscience.com/tours

GO GLOBAL,
VISIT THE MAPPARIUM

Ever dreamed of walking clear across the world? Well, here's your chance to do it. The Mary Baker Eddy Library holds within its walls a thirty-foot, vividly stained glass globe designed by architect Chester Lindsay Churchill back in 1935 and called the "Mapparium." The low-lit, perfectly spherical chamber depicts the geographical and geopolitical standings of that year, and to this date it has never been updated, which means that the Mapparium presents history buffs with the opportunity to see the world as it was before the start of the second World War. Three times every hour, visitors are permitted inside to check out its many exciting features; among them, acoustical tricks. Say something directly beneath the North Star and hear yourself speak in surround sound. Grab a partner, stand at opposite ends of the central footbridge, and whisper something sweet; your partner will be the only person to hear it.

200 Massachusetts Ave., Boston, 617-450-7000
www.mbelibrary.org

TIP

Mary Baker Eddy founded the Christian Science religious movement of the late nineteenth century, and the Mapparium is just one part of the much larger Christian Science Plaza. Also on campus, First Church of Christ, Scientist's Mother Church (page 97).

LOOK FOR ART
AT THE LIBRARY

The Boston Public Library's printed collections certainly make it a boon for readers and researchers in this city and beyond, but did you know its Central Library in Copley Square is not only a repository of books? Visitors encounter incredible art at every turn, beginning with the Dartmouth Street vestibule's sculpted bronze doors by Daniel Chester French (the artist who did the Lincoln Memorial in Washington, DC) and moving on to allegorical murals by French painter Chavannes. And there's John Singer Sargent's monumental *Triumph of Religion* cycle, an extraordinary offering from an artist more widely known for his portraiture. Get the full creative scoop on free art and architecture tours that are offered daily, or stop in at your leisure and just walk around.

Central Branch, 700 Boylston St., Boston, 617-536-5400
www.bpl.org

TIP

In fair weather, pack your own
lunch, or buy it at one of the
food trucks in Copley Square, and have
a picnic in the library's open-air inner
courtyard. The marble arcade
and dappling fountain set a
serene tone. Those in the know
come often to read and relax.

BE A CHURCHGOER
AT TRINITY

Wondering what that behemoth of a stone building is in Copley Square? If you guessed church, you're right; it's Trinity Church. You must go to at least one Sunday morning service here in your lifetime. It's a spiritual experience, whether you're religious or not. The choir sings from the altar; the sanctuary glows with gold tones and rich color. Sitting in the pews, parishioners read the words "Blessing and honor and glory" up on the transept, and it feels right. Dedicated in 1877, Trinity Church offers one of the first and finest examples of American-born design. Take a guided tour of Trinity (or self-guide) to learn about the building's magnificent Richardsonian Romanesque architecture, the congregation's rock-star nineteenth-century preacher Phillip Brooks, and the incredible art—much of it created by John La Farge. Tours are free on Sundays immediately after the service. Otherwise, it's $7.

206 Clarendon St., 617-536-0944
www.trinitychurchboston.org

GET SCHOOLED
IN CONTEMPORARY ART

Henry Moore, Jaume Plensa, Frank Stella, Mark di Suvero . . . .
Think I'm sending you to a contemporary art museum? Nope.
On the contrary, you're headed over to the campus at MIT—
that's right, the world's foremost technology university—to
appreciate stellar works by many of the heavy hitters of twentieth-
century sculpture. Not to be forgotten are art and architecture
greats, including Sol LeWitt and Frank Gehry. MIT's public art
collection of more than fifty pieces is a little-known secret among
locals. Walk around the Kendall Square campus and check it out
for yourself. Don't forget your iPhone—in true MIT style, each
piece contains a QR code that you can scan to learn more.

Cambridge, 617-253-4680
listart.mit.edu/collections/public-art-collection

SEE ART
AT THE MFA...

Just because you're browsing fine art doesn't mean you have to dress like a well-heeled collector, so strap on your sneakers for this art adventure because you'll need them. You could spend a week roaming the galleries of the goliath Museum of Fine Arts Boston and not come across the same work twice. It's Boston's answer to Paris's Louvre and New York's Met. Key attractions include ancient Egyptian funerary art (mummies, too), the Impressionist Gallery with almost three dozen paintings including Monet's *Water Lilies* and Renoir's *Dance at Bougival*, and the monastic-styled Buddhist Temple Room featuring *Dainichi, Buddha of Infinite Illumination*. Make sure to check out the fifty-three galleries (gah!) in the modern Art of the Americas wing, with relics from the Pre-Columbian era and Paul Revere's *Sons of Liberty Bowl*.

465 Huntington Ave., Boston, 617-267-9300

www.mfa.org

...AND THEN
DRAW SOME

You don't have to have an artistic bone in your body to have fun at the MFA's weekly Drawing in the Galleries event. It's like Paint Nite without the cost—or, unfortunately, the wine, but you can grab a glass after. Every Wednesday night from 6-9 p.m. the museum provides sketching materials (pencils, paper, clipboards) and an instructor for free in one of its galleries. Location rotates by week, which means you could end up shading in the perfectly sculpted abs of a marble male torso from the Roman Imperial period in the Art of the Ancient World galleries or a live model posing in front of a Jackson Pollock. Did I mention that the museum also offers free admission on Wednesday after 4:45 p.m.? So now you really have no excuse not to check this out, and then, of course, enjoy that wine.

465 Huntington Ave., Boston, 617-267-9300
www.mfa.org

VISIT HER PALAZZO,
ISABELLA STEWART
GARDNER MUSEUM

This might be Boston's most talked-about hidden gem. The Isabella Stewart Gardner Museum opened in 1903 to show off the personal art collection of Gardner, a wealthy local gentlewoman and lover of the arts. From the start it was one hot gathering place for the day's emerging artists and writers, including John Singer Sargent and Henry James. Today, as then, visitors take in the pieces Gardner gathered on multiple trips to Europe, Asia, and beyond—items such as Rembrandt's *Self Portrait* and Titian's *Europa*—in small, salon-style rooms. Perhaps its biggest calling card is the building itself, commissioned by Gardner at the turn of the century to replicate a fifteenth-century Venetian palace, complete with cloisters, balconies, and a simply stunning interior courtyard that is meticulously dressed with blooming flowers 365 days per year.

25 Evans Way, Boston, 617-566-1401, 617-278-5156 (box office)
www.gardnermuseum.org

TIP

Wear your Red Sox gear
for a $2 discount off admission.
Did you know? Isabella Gardner
was a huge fan of her hometown
baseball team and often showed
her support publicly.

LACE UP YOUR SNEAKERS
AND WALK THE FREEDOM TRAIL

Don't snub this taken-for-granted Boston history adventure. The fifty-year-old walking trail marked by bricks and red paint is a widely recognized must for tourists, but it's surprising how few local Bostonians have attempted the two-and-a-half mile jaunt. Guide-led organized tours offer snapshots in short, or visitors can walk it themselves with a map in hand to unearth the full chronicle of each of its sixteen historic sites. Those of you who are up for the challenge can feel the lumpy curves of cobblestones underfoot and imagine you're living in the age of Paul Revere, John Hancock, John Adams, and Samuel Adams. You're still subjects of England, but tensions between Patriots and Loyalists are high. Roam a few early cemeteries with their tightly packed and fantastically graphic grave markers; visit the 1729 Old South Meeting House, a Puritan church and public gathering place for revolutionaries; climb the 221-foot Bunker Hill Monument, which looks a lot like Washington DC's Washington Monument. Near the trail's conclusion in Charlestown, the USS *Constitution* warship— still commissioned by the Navy and one of the Freedom Trail's most visited sites—is undergoing restoration in dry dock through 2018.

Starting point: Boston Common Visitor Center
139 Tremont St., Boston, 617-357-8300
www.thefreedomtrail.org

● ●

SUSS OUT THE FUSS
ABOUT FANEUIL HALL

It's a Boston icon. It's one of America's top tourist attractions. It's famously known as the "Cradle of Liberty." So, what's all the fuss about? In case you don't know, Faneuil Hall is only one of the most important buildings in the history of this country. During the eighteenth century, it acted as an open food market and Boston's town hall, then quickly turned into a hangout for rebels fighting British empirical rule—yep, James Otis, Samuel Adams, and the like. After the war, the Hall remained a place of protest for national hot-button issues like slavery and women's suffrage, frequently hosting prominent speakers like Frederick Douglass and Susan B. Anthony. Today, it's a visitor center and the headquarters of Boston National Historical Park. Spend a couple bucks on souvenirs at the first floor shops, but don't miss the hall's upstairs offerings—many do. Patriotic art decorates the second floor Great Hall, including a charcoal-sketched standing portrait of Abraham Lincoln by artist William Morris Hunt that was discovered onsite in the 1990s hidden behind another of Hunt's works. On the fourth floor, the Armory and Museum of The Ancient & Honorable Artillery Company shows off loads of military artifacts from all wars, like full dress epaulets, Confederate copper powder flasks, and a waistcoat worn by Dr. Joseph Warren who was killed during the Battle of Bunker Hill.

1 Faneuil Hall Square, Boston, 617-242-5642

www.nps.gov/bost

PAY YOUR RESPECTS
TO PAUL REVERE

Oft mentioned in the same breath as Samuel Adams, John Hancock, and Joseph Warren, Paul Revere exists as one of the Revolutionary Era's grandest personalities, thanks to his midnight ride, made famous in Longfellow's titular poem. But Revere was neither statesman nor Founding Father; he was a modest local entrepreneur who pitched in for the cause. Nonetheless, we are talking about Paul Revere here, the father of sixteen, the man who touched many a Boston landmark with his craft (including the Massachusetts State House and the USS *Constitution*), the artisan whose silver pieces stand for the early American decorative arts movement and have been placed in the holdings of many fine art museums. Pay tribute to his life at his final resting place within the wrought-iron-fenced Granary Burying Ground. By our New World standards it's an ancient place, established in 1660—by the time Revere died at eighty-three, it was already more than 150 years old. Spend a moment and drop a penny at the diminutive slate stone that simply reads "Revere's Tomb."

Granary Burying Ground, Tremont Street at Park Street, 617-635-4505

TREK TO LEARN
BLACK HISTORY

Explore Boston's other freedom trail. Less known but no less important than its Revolutionary-War-themed counterpart, the Black Heritage Trail guides you past sites significant in Boston's African American legacy. It also juts through the heart of Beacon Hill, past Charles Street's chichi boutiques—so bring your spending money—and past John Kerry's home base in Louisburg Square. The trail's reach extends much farther back than the Civil War; in fact, slavery had been abolished in the Commonwealth by 1783. Pick up a map at the Museum of African American History on Joy Street and start walking. Along the way, see the Lewis Hayden House, a station on the Underground Railroad and a meeting place for abolitionists: the Abiel Smith School, built in 1835 to educate black children; and the African Meeting House, built at the turn of the nineteenth century by free blacks, the oldest surviving of its kind in the U.S.

Starting point: Abiel Smith School, 46 Joy St., Boston, 617-742-5415
www.nps.gov/boaf

SALUTE
THIS HISTORIC SHIP

Ahoy, mate. Join the throngs of 500,000 trekking to Charlestown Navy Yard this year to see the USS *Constitution* in all her glory and you'll get a different-than-usual encounter—at least until 2018. Old Ironsides is de-rigged and in dry dock for restoration, but you can still see some of this Freedom Trail attraction. History buffs can get their groove on with a photo op on the Constitution's top deck and then converse with official Navy crew tasked with talking about our favorite ship of state. Did you know that George Washington named her? That she was one of the Navy's first six ships? That she never lost a battle? Ever. And she fought plenty of them over her 58 years of active duty, including epic battles during the War of 1812. As a result of this out-of-water experience, a few rare opportunities arise. You can view her entire hull, including the portions that normally sit below the waterline. In addition, visitors to the adjacent USS Constitution Museum (free to get in!) can sign messages and their names to real copper sheaths that will ultimately be attached to the hull for protection until future restorations—like, in at least 20 years!

Charlestown Navy Yard, Pier 1, Charlestown, 617-799-8198
www.navy.mil/local/constitution

TIP

From downtown Boston, the easiest way to get to the Navy Yard is actually by sea. Take the MBTA's Commuter Boat—ten minutes and a gorgeous view of the North End for $3.25.

GO COLONIAL
CRYPT HOPPING

Indulge your macabre inclination with this twofer that puts a mildly grotesque spin on Freedom Trail history.

Behind-the-Scenes Tour

Another Loyalist house of worship, Old North Church, also opens its crypt for viewing, but this tour is not nearly as macabre an experience. For starters, Old North has a modern basement, despite being the oldest-standing church building in Boston. Three dozen tombs serve as the final resting places for 1,100 people, one level beneath the creaky floorboards of the sanctuary. British Major John Pitcairn, Ann Ruggles, and William Shippard are among the figures buried here, but the most famous is Samuel Nicholson, the first captain of the USS *Constitution*, who still receives visitors every year.

193 Salem St., Boston, 617-858-8231
www.oldnorth.com

Bells and Bones Tour

New England's first Anglican church, King's Chapel, offers this tour for a nominal fee, daily, in season. Interim Director Lucas Griswold guides you around back and through an iron-gated archway into the stone basement of the church. Here lie twenty-one tombs filled with approximately 100 to 150 bodies (a jumble of bones) of eighteenth-century Boston's top political tier. The Bulfinch family owned Tomb 1, where famous architect Charles rested for about a decade until his family moved his remains to Mt. Auburn Cemetery. Tomb 9 was owned by Charles Paxton, the city's Commissioner of Customs before the Revolution. Don't miss the Coolidge family tomb (the ancestors of Calvin Coolidge), which has a brick removed from its front, allowing you a peek inside where you will see grisly bits. If you're afraid of the dark, proceed with caution. After resurfacing from the cellar, if the weather cooperates and you haven't had your knees replaced, climb King's bell tower where the largest and last bronze bell cast by Paul Revere still rings.

58 Tremont St., Boston, 617-523-1749
www.kings-chapel.org

HITCH A RIDE
THROUGH HISTORY

Hop on the MBTA's Green Line for the shortest subway ride of your life, but a darn historic one. The MBTA is America's oldest public transit system. At Park Street Station, your point of departure, let your gaze wander over Lilli Ann Rosenberg's tile mosaic which celebrates the Tremont Street Subway. What's this? Only the oldest subway tunnel in North America, down which you're about to careen onboard a modern streetcar—hold on tight for the squeal. Get off at Boylston Street. It's the next station, and you could probably run the distance on foot in under a minute. Why so soon? Boylston is the oldest underground transit station in the U.S. and has remained largely unchanged since it opened in 1897. It's also a museum of sorts: train addicts can get their fix over by the Type 5 Semiconvertible and a 1950 PCC Model, which are both on display at the inbound platform. And there you have it. One big bang for two bucks and ten cents.

Park Street Station, Tremont Street at Park Street,
Boylston Street Station, Tremont Street at Boylston Street,
617-222-3200
www.mbta.com

FIND FAMOUS
DEAD FOLKS AND SO MUCH MORE

Take a walk in a park—well, the 175-acre Mount Auburn Cemetery, christened a "rural cemetery and experimental garden" in 1831 and America's first large-scale, designed green space. Contrary to popular belief, Mount Auburn was not planned by famous landscape architect Frederick Law Olmsted, who would have been just nine years old in 1831. Mount Auburn actually inspired Olmsted's and others' future park creations—including New York's Central Park. While Mount Auburn remains an active place of burial, there's lots more to do here than hang out with famous dead people. For one, it's an accredited arboretum with more than 800 individual species of trees. Seasonally, it is home to exotic migratory birds (bring your binoculars!). Ultimately, history/literature/politics buffs can check out the sunny final resting places of such distinguished folk as Henry Cabot Lodge, Dorothea Dix, Fanny Farmer, Nathaniel Bowditch, Henry Wadsworth Longfellow, Charles Bulfinch, B.F. Skinner, and Mary Baker Eddy. In the nineteenth century, Mount Auburn was the country's most popular tourist attraction, excluding Niagara Falls; today, it welcomes 250,000 visitors annually.

580 Mount Auburn St., Cambridge, 617-547-7105
www.mountauburn.org

SEEK OUT
TWO PILLARS OF CAMELOT

Boston should think about renaming Columbia Point as Kennedy Point, now that it's home to both the John F. Kennedy Presidential Library and Museum (renovated in 2015) and the Edward M. Kennedy Institute for the U.S. Senate (new in 2015). The late former president and senator are two of Massachusetts's favorite sons, and each had an overwhelming effect on American politics. Learn about hot-button issues of the 1960s at the Museum—including the Cuban Missile Crisis and the Space Race—and garner some insight on JFK's personal and family life. The Institute focuses on politics today with a full-scale reproduction of the U.S. Senate Chamber and interactive exploration of the legislative process.

Edward M. Kennedy Institute, 210 Morrissey Blvd., Boston, 617-740-7000
www.emkinstitute.org

John F. Kennedy Presidential Library and Museum, Columbia Point,
Boston, 617-514-1600
www.jfklibrary.org

EXPERIENCE
HARVARD'S FLOWER POWER

When asked to cite a significant artist working in glass, the name Dale Chihuly might spring to mind—at least if you're anybody who knows anything about art. But famous as Chihuly is these days, he's not the most famous glass artist in Boston. That title goes to Leopold Blaschka and his son Rudolph, the two men responsible for Harvard Museum of Natural History's Ware Collection of Glass Models of Plants, a.k.a. the Glass Flowers. This 3,000-piece collection details 847 different plant species and, incredibly, does so with scientific accuracy. In the 1880s, Harvard botany professor George Lincoln Goodale commissioned the German-born Blaschkas—then known for their glass models of invertebrate marine animals—to create a few replicas by hand for use in teaching students about botany and for filling the display cases of his new museum. The colorful, precise, extraordinary flora facsimiles on exhibit today were created over a course of fifty years. Chihuly was quoted as calling them "mind-boggling," but I say they can't accurately be described on paper. Go see them for yourself!

26 Oxford St., Cambridge, 617-495-3045
www.hmnh.harvard.edu

EXPLORE THE LORE
OF HARVARD YARD

Can you, or can't you "pahk ya cah in Hahvahd Yahd"? This famous factoid is not the only one needing closer inspection on the campus of the country's oldest university. While you stroll the paths of the Old Yard, wander under its two-dozen-plus gates and imagine you're one of the world's most elite thinkers. Then try to identify an inaccuracy here that's been rather permanently etched in stone, er, bronze. No takers? Oh, I'll just tell you: in front of University Hall, Daniel Chester French's iconic statue of John Harvard is also known as the Statue of the Three Lies. Why? Its inscription reads "John Harvard, Founder, 1638." False, false, and false. Harvard University was established as the New College in 1636 by a vote of the colonial court, while Harvard himself was still living in jolly old England. It bears his name because upon his death in Charlestown in 1638, he bequeathed a portion of his estate and library to the school. Lastly, no one has any idea what John Harvard looked like; French created the statue almost 250 years after Harvard's death and used a model to do so, because there weren't any known portraits of the benefactor. Here's to *Veritas*!

Cambridge, 617-495-1000
www.harvard.edu

COLLEGES & UNIVERSITIES
IN THE HUB OF THE UNIVERSE

It's no secret that Boston's got loads of schools and, consequently, loads of well-educated people. Did you know that there are more than 50 colleges and universities in the general metropolitan region? In case you need convincing that Harvard's not the only game in town, here's my short list of major players:

- Bentley University
- Berklee College of Music
- Boston College
- Boston Conservatory
- Boston University
- Brandeis University
- Bunker Hill Community College
- Emerson College
- Emmanuel College
- Harvard University
- Lesley University
- Massachusetts College of Art and Design
- Massachusetts Institute of Technology
- New England Conservatory
- Northeastern University
- Simmons College
- Suffolk University
- Tufts University
- UMASS Boston
- Wentworth Institute of Technology

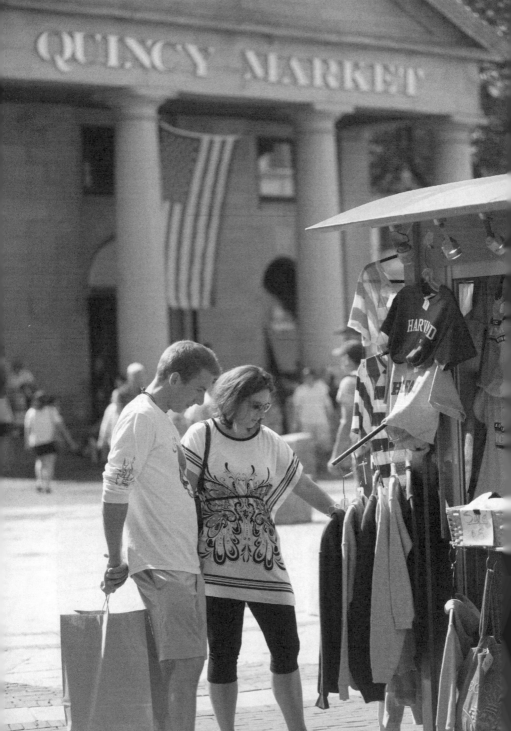

SHOPPING AND FASHION

BROWSE THE STACKS
AT BRATTLE BOOK SHOP

Ken Gloss' old-time Brattle Book Shop might be a hot spot for antiquarian books, but there's nothing dusty, musty, or fusty about this bookstore. What it is: jam-packed floor to ceiling with reads of every variety and every era since Johannes Gutenberg printed his first Bible. Looking for some light reading? Pick up last year's *The New York Times* best seller. It is likely stacked next to a work of fiction from the nineteenth-century—Gloss doesn't classify by age but rather by genre, and these range from Foreign Travel to Theology & Philosophy to General World History to a whole bookcase on Firefighting. For the truly dedicated, the experience gets real up on the third floor where Brattle houses its rare book room and, for bibliomaniacs, each visit yields a treasure.

9 West St., Boston, 617-542-0210
www.brattlebookshop.com

HEAD TO MARKET, TO MARKET
[SOUTH END OPEN MARKET @ SoWa, THAT IS]

Treasure hunt time! Whether you're looking for antiques or contemporary crafts made by local artisans, your best bet for finding something seriously cool exists at the South End Open Market @ SoWa. Blocks of vendors hawk jewelry, soap, doggie capes, and everything in between. Farmers and food makers congregate in a special corner selling seasonal produce, cheeses, and fresh baked goods. Be sure to block off a few hours for exploration and don't worry about bringing lunch—there's always a food truck rally with upwards of twenty different options.

May through October

460-540 Harrison Ave., Boston
www.newenglandopenmarkets.com

GET YOUR SMART ON
AT HARVARD BOOK STORE

This place is a crack house for book junkies. It's where the Harvard community pops in for recreational and academic reading materials and where the rest of us ordinary Joes go to study up—and yet we must go. The sheer amount of literature that eighty-plus-year-old independent retailer Harvard Book Store shelves on just about every topic is overwhelming: food writing, art history, gender studies, mystery, "lit crit," Western philosophy. Stop in, look around, climb a wall-mounted wooden ladder for a better view of the top of the stacks. Then go downstairs to the used and remaindered department, where titles are marked forty to eighty percent off list price.

1256 Massachusetts Ave., Cambridge, 617-661-1515
www.harvard.com

TIP

Harvard Book Store's evening author events are legendary, attracting writers from former presidents to Pulitzer Prize winners. Usually they're free.

PRETEND
YOU'RE PRETTY WOMAN

Don't we all wish we could shop 'til we drop with Richard
Gere's credit card? In lieu of that ever happening, channel Julia
Roberts and window shop—unless you've got serious cash to
burn—in Newbury Street's first two blocks, between Arlington
and Clarendon cross streets. This is prime real estate for high
fashion Italian, French, and American designer boutiques. It's
Boston's Rodeo Drive.

Burberry
2 Newbury St., Boston, 617-236-1000

Tiffany & Co.
5 Newbury St., Boston, 617-217-5778

Chanel
6 Newbury St., Boston, 617-859-0055

Dolce & Gabbana
11 Newbury St., Boston, 857-254-0668

Giorgio Armani
22 Newbury St., Boston, 617-267-3200

Cartier
40 Newbury St., Boston, 617-262-3300

Loro Piana
43 Newbury St., Boston, 617-236-4999

Valentino
47 Newbury St., Boston, 617-578-0300

MaxMara
69 Newbury St., Boston, 617-267-9775

Diane von Furstenberg
73 Newbury St., Boston, 617-247-7300

Ralph Lauren
93-95 Newbury St., Boston, 617-424-1124

www.newbury-st.com

BUY INTO ART
IN SoWa

You definitely won't stumble upon SoWa unless you're lost. The enclave (named for being South of Washington Street) is tucked on the far side of the South End by Interstate 93, and it's full of rundown warehouses. Over the last decade, artists and designers have been slowly revitalizing the area, and today it is one of the city's most creative 'hoods. Head over there and wander through a cornucopia of artist studios, art galleries, design firms, and all-sorts-of-creative shops. Fashion-forward individuals gravitate to Galvin-ized Headwear, Peng, and December Thieves. Find art books at Ars Libri and home decor imports at Mohr & McPherson or Goosefish Press letterpress shop. More than two dozen galleries show off the latest work of emerging and established contemporary artists. A good way to tap this scene is through monthly First Friday gatherings, free and open to anyone. Start at Thayer Street and Harrison Ave.

Bounded by Shawmut Avenue and Albany Street
www.sowaboston.com

STOCK UP
YOUR STETSON COLLECTION

Bobby From Boston is Boston's answer to New York City thrift shopping, and this place is so vintage that you won't find anything made after the 1960s hanging on the racks. Bobby's South End store spotlights menswear for the most part. A dapper display of Dobbs and Stetson felt fedoras and homburgs brings to mind Winston Churchill or Don Draper. Skinny ties and bow ties, tie clips and cuff links, inlaid pocket knives and black-and-white wing tips; each find is unique. A rear room pleases ladies, with one-of-a-kind frocks from the first half of the twentieth century as well as clunky, chunky platform heels and beaded clutch bags. Hollywood film costumers sourcing period clothing call in often—it's silver screen cool.

19 Thayer St., Boston, 617-423-9299

PREPARE A PIPE
A LA HARVARD'S OLD GUARD

Welcome to nineteenth-century Harvard's "den of sin" (according to those of a puritanical mindset). Why all the infamy? Well, for its billiards tables, abundant stash of tobacco, and reputation for being selectively exclusive. Fast forward about 130 years and Leavitt & Peirce continues to curate a tobacco bar that's so top-notch people travel to buy from it. Just across the way from the university's yard, the independent smoke shop sports an old-timey vibe, an iconic storefront, and products you may have seen in historical dramas (or Harvard yearbooks)—pipes, straight razors, shave brushes, cribbage boards, and other games. Leave it to Ivy Leaguers to support tradition, right?

1316 Massachusetts Ave., Cambridge, 617-547-0576
www.leavitt-peirce.com

BOUTIQUE SHOP
IN BEACON HILL

If you're looking to avoid the steep, high-fashion prices of Newbury Street, go check out Charles Street in Beacon Hill. Don't get me wrong, things aren't cheap in this historically Brahmin neighborhood, but you won't have to worry about falling in love with a $5,000 Chanel LBD, either. Shops along this half-mile stretch are absolutely adorable, both inside and out front, and they typically fall into two categories: antiques and independent boutiques. I have too many favorites to mention them all, so instead I offer my Charles Street CliffsNotes.

Flat of the Hill
60 Charles St., Boston
617-619-9977
www.flatofthehill.com

Black Ink
101 Charles St., Boston
617-723-3883
www.blackinkboston.com

Savenor's
160 Charles St., Boston
617-723-6328
www.savenorsmarket.com

Twentieth Century Limited
73 Charles St., Boston, 617-742-1031
www.boston-vintagejewelry.com

Danish Country
138 Charles St., Boston
617-227-1804
www.danishcountry.net

Helen's Leather
110 Charles St., Boston
617-742-2077
www.helensleather.com

NRO Kids
126 Charles St., Boston
617-742-0009
www.northriveroutfitter.com

Holiday
53 Charles St., Boston
617-973-9730
www.holidayboutique.net

OLD-WORLD MARKET HOP
IN THE NORTH END

Your mission: shop Boston's little slice of Italy and return with flavorful, authentic (yes, really!) food items that you would never, ever, ever find at a mega mart.

Polcari's

Located on the corner of Richmond and Salem streets, Polcari's is the picture of the old-world general store. It's a bit dark inside, but not at all unfriendly; in fact, the owners work the counter and greet North End regulars in native Italian. Bags of dried chamomile and Ceylon cinnamon inspire you to make tea at home—much more fragrant than the supermarket variety. You can also pic k up spices and coffee by the pound.

105 Salem St., Boston, 617-227-0786
www.polcariscoffee.com

Salumeria Italiana

If you like to cook with ingredients imported from the boot, Salumeria Italiana is your stop. Find fresh pasta varieties, jars of bruschetta toppings, spreads, prepared tomatoes, Illy coffee, premium olive oils, and balsamic vinegars. There's also a deli counter with imported Italian meats and cheeses, as well as olives, salted capers, roasted peppers, and more. Calabrese soppressata, anyone?

151 Richmond St., Boston, 617-523-8743
www.salumeriaitaliana.com

Bova's Bakery

Bova's should be your stop for sweets. You'll have to venture off Hanover and away from the Italian bakeries of guidebook fame to find it, but when you do, it's guaranteed to be open—twenty-four hours a day. Locally, it's famous for its fresh Italian bread, which you can smell baking in the wee hours, but you can't overlook the pastries, literally: the display cases are jammed with them, authentic Italian and otherwise. My favorite are the lemon snowballs, and they also come flavored with anise.

134 Salem St., Boston, 617-523-5601
www.bovabakeryboston.com

Cirace's

Finds at the Richmond Street liquor store Cirace's include all the Italian specialties, from grappa and limoncello to vin santo and Italian dessert wine. The owners offer a printed beginners' guide to their amari selection, which is comprehensive enough to warrant one. Wine lovers, like myself, have a blast perusing the room devoted to Italian wine separated by region.

173 North St., Boston, 617-227-3193
www.vcirace.com

GET GEAR TO CHEER
AT RED SOX TEAM STORE

'47 Brand's massive apparel and souvenir store across the street from Fenway Park makes it easy to root, root, root for the home team. For starters, the place features hundreds of baseball caps in one room, from adjustable and snapback to knit, all emblazoned with the team's famous "B." Traditional jerseys, fashion-cut tanks, and baby sweatshirts occupy a second room, while a third, named Red Sox Clubhouse, hawks "real" items like bricks and seat backs from Fenway, autographed baseballs, and framed infield dirt from the 2014 World Series—that's a Sox fan's dream come true.

19 Yawkey Way, Boston, 800-336-9299
www.yawkeywaystore.com

MAKE LIKE A TOURIST
AT FANEUIL HALL MARKETPLACE

Although its roster of stores may read like a mall directory, this historic marketplace is one of Boston's most popular tourist destinations. It's worthy of a shopping trip for its independent boutiques as well as pushcarts purveying hyper-local goods inside and immediately surrounding the Quincy Market Building. The open-air concourse gets its name from the famous landmark, Faneuil Hall, at its western end. Stop here for a casual lunch with the kids, but be warned that multiple tabs from the massive food colonnade add up fast. Then, if your bank isn't totally bust, consider Ghirardelli for gooey gourmet ice cream sundaes. When Boston's weather doesn't get too hairy, performance artists entertain the throngs with circus acts like juggling, improv dance moves, and magic tricks.

Confined by Congress, State and North streets and Surface Road, Boston
617-523-1300
www.faneuilhallmarketplace.com

ACTIVITIES
BY SEASON

• •

SUGGESTED
ITINERARIES

CLASSIC BOSTON

FUN FOR THE KIDDOS

FODDER FOR HISTORY BUFFS

● ●

EVERY FOODIE'S FANTASY

STYLE MAVENS APPLY HERE

• •

SPORTS, SPORTS, SPORTS

OUTDOOR ADDICTS

FOR THE CREATIVE CREW

• •

©Alexandra Molnar for Massachusetts Office of Travel and Tourism

INDEX

• •

144